when the
wind blows...

Our working lives are shaped by many forces.
What matters is how we react to them.

some people
build walls

We can simply accept – or even resist –
the influences and opportunities that come our way.

others build
windmills

Or we can take control and turn them to our own advantage.

In today's world of work,
the wind is blowing harder...
and changing direction more
frequently than before.

That brings more problems for the
person who builds walls...
but even greater rewards for the
person who builds windmills.

This book will help you master the art of
taking control of your own career –
and shaping the kind of life you choose.

Facing a world of change…

Not long ago career paths were narrowly defined – often for life.

But today, we all face constant change.

New kinds of companies arise and new patterns of work evolve. And the global market and ever-developing technology go on creating endless new possibilities.

Narrow, one-dimensional job roles have given way to today's self-reliant, flexible, multi-skilled, IT-competent teamworker.

Yet many people fail to appreciate the extent of these changes – often because job titles have stayed the same.

To stay employable in the future, you need to adapt to new roles, gain new skills and master new ways of building a career.

And the best way is to take control of the forces that shape our working lives and turn them to your advantage.

JUST THINK…
you could spend at least 40 years of 40 weeks and 40 hours a week in employment. That's a long time to be stuck in a job or career you can't stand! Yet, incredibly, most people devote more time to planning their annual holiday than to thinking about a whole lifetime in work.

HOW DO YOU SEE SUCCESS?
It's worth spending a little time thinking about just what you want from life. For instance, some people need a steady job, others thrive on change. You may work to live – using it to finance your real interests. Or you may live for your work and see career satisfaction as your true goal.

WHAT DO YOU WANT IN LIFE?

These new challenges also mean exciting new opportunities.

Once it took years to achieve recognition, responsibility and financial rewards.

Today the influences and opportunities in our lives are more powerful and varied. The rewards can also be much greater – and success can come much quicker.

But what do we mean by success? This should be your first question.

After all, we all take our own pathway through our working and learning life – and we all have our own goals.

Whatever your ideal job or your life objectives, the key is to manage your career in a way that lets you achieve them.

…you need to take control

'The Art of Building Windmills' will reveal how to position yourself for success by mastering *action thinking*.
This dynamic technique ensures that you – and nobody else – are in control of your career. It lets you spot (or even create) opportunities as they arise – and then seize them.

You'll find *action thinking* explained fully in **Tactic 5**. But first you'll learn about the other vital **Tactics** you need to make your *action thinking* effective:

Tactic 1 identifies the skills you have (and need).

Tactic 2 lets you discover where you want to go in life.

Tactic 3 reveals a wealth of hidden opportunities.

Tactic 4 explains the best ways to sell yourself to employers.

And then, having mastered *action thinking*, **Tactic 6** explains the career-boosting techniques of making your present job work for you, thinking laterally and becoming an expert networker.

Finally, **Tactic 7** helps you check how well you're managing your career.

USE IT THE BEST WAY FOR YOU

If you choose to follow this sequence, the book provides a comprehensive step-by-step guide to taking charge of your career.

Alternatively, you'll find it just as useful to dip in and out as you choose.

And if there's an area where you need special help, the at-a-glance guide on the next page will point you in the right direction.

NOW TAKE CONTROL!

The secret is to take control of your own career – and shape the kind of life *you* choose.

Managing your career is a super-skill in itself and requires new career management tactics.

RELAX!
Don't worry if there seems a lot to do – just one idea could be all you need to put you on track for success.

YOUR BIG PLUS
Once you understand the nature of the new world of work, you have a major advantage. And this book will help you make the most of it.

Where are you now?

Do you need to:

- Understand your strengths and marketability?
- Make sure you don't undersell yourself?

- Discover what really motivates you?
- Give your career more focus and direction?

- Know how to work towards the right job for you?
- Open up exciting new career possibilities?

- Improve your CV and interview techniques?
- Boost your self-confidence?

- Learn how to position yourself for opportunities?
- Become more employable and satisfied in your career?

- Master the short cuts to success?
- Give your career a boost?

- Check and improve your new career skills?
- Keep on moving forward in life?

T7

Contents

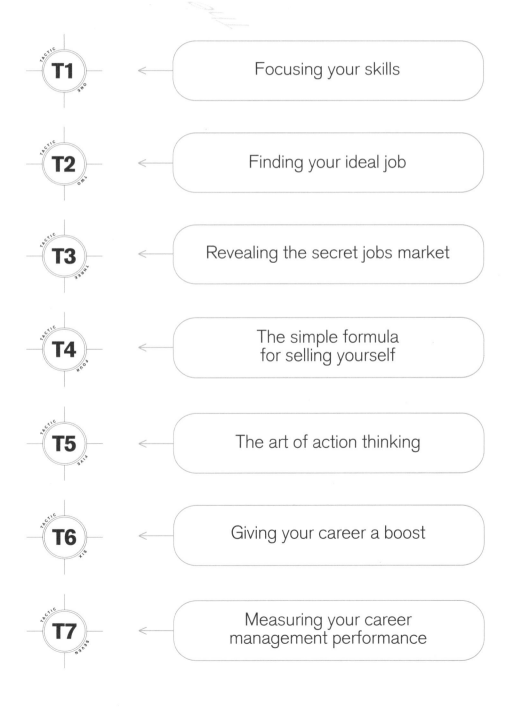

How the book works…

Reading books can be hard work – and having to take action is even harder.

That's why we've structured this book to make it easy.

You can see at a glance where you are up to – and what you need to do next.

Each of the *Tactics* contains three sections. These are colour-coded blue, green and orange.

READ · *Read –* This outlines the ideas that will help you succeed – so it's the first thing you need to *read*!
It also prepares you to *act* on these ideas and refers you to the research material and exercises which will help you *think* about the ideas in more detail.

THINK · *Think –* This reference section contains more detailed research material and exercises which you will often need to check.

ACT · *Act! –* These sections tell you how to put the ideas into action.

From reading the blue section, you'll have a good idea of what actions will be needed.

However, you will be referred all the time to the green *think* section to provide the detailed information to help you create your action prompts.

To help you work through the process make sure you keep a notebook or file to hand. We suggest you jot down brief notes on the actions needed as you tackle each **Tactic**. These will then build up step by step into a comprehensive set of action prompts.

And finally, bear in mind that to gain maximum benefit from 'The Art of Building Windmills' you will need to complete all the **Tactics** *– the whole is greater than the sum of the parts.*

REMEMBER
READ, THINK
and, above all, ACT!
It's your career –
nobody else's!

focusing your skills

T1

TACTIC ONE

to be **employed** is to be at **risk**, to be **employable** is to be **secure**

Focusing your skills

In this *Tactic* you will discover how to:

- **Check your portfolio of skills**
- **Focus on the ones you need to develop**

We've already looked at the dramatic changes in the world of work.

Naturally these changes demand a whole new mix of skills and attributes.

Once you understand what is needed, you have a head start in today's fast-changing employment scene.

CHECK YOUR SKILLS

Analysis of five years of national employer surveys suggests the desired skills fall into four broad areas:

1 SELF-RELIANCE SKILLS

Self-management • Self-awareness
Proactivity • Willingness to learn
Self-promotion • Networking • Planning action

2 PEOPLE SKILLS

Teamworking • Interpersonal skills • Oral communication
Leadership • Customer orientation • Foreign language

3 GENERAL SKILLS

Problem-solving • Flexibility • Business acumen
IT/computer literacy • Numeracy • Commitment

4 SPECIALIST SKILLS

Occupational skills • Technical skills
Understanding commercial goals • Company-related expertise
Professional expertise • Strategic planning skills

MAKE SURE...
[1] You use the most relevant examples of these skills when applying for your next job or project.
[2] You review your skills regularly and recognise how 'portable' they are.
[3] Start thinking 'I *can* do' rather than simply 'I do'.

So how employable are you?

In other words, how does your present portfolio of skills measure up against this profile?

To check this you need to:

Map out your skills by listing your experiences and achievements.

Collect the evidence that proves you have these skills.

Review your skills, assess which are strongest, which you enjoy using most and which you need to develop.

When assessing your existing skills, take care not to undersell yourself.

Many of us fail to realise what skills we possess and just take our abilities for granted.

This one-dimensional approach means we often focus only on skills and experience gained from traditional full-time paid work.

To avoid this, you should map out a detailed profile of all the areas of your life.

Look at all dimensions: full-time work, part-time work, voluntary work, home work, community work.

To help you *think* about this, try looking at the following sections.

Check your balance of skills

The following exercise encourages you to think about your key skills and attributes.

It will boost your awareness of your strengths and areas for development so you can:

- **Improve** your chances of achieving your ideal job (see **Tactic 2**)

- **Promote** yourself more effectively (see **Tactic 4**)

- **Assess** ways of increasing your employability (see **Tactic 6**)

MAPPING OUT YOUR SKILLS

1. **List** the positive experiences and achievements in your career to date.

   If you are already in work this is not too difficult. But think too about experiences in part-time work, voluntary work and work undertaken for social purposes, eg for clubs, community groups or similar organisations.

2. **Look at** the list of words in the skills portfolio (overleaf) and recognise skills and attributes that have resulted from (1).

3. **Put yourself in the shoes** of three people in turn – eg friends/family, tutors/lecturers, people you have worked for, people you work with, and other work-related contacts. How would their views of you differ? You could even ask those people to do it for you – make them promise to be honest.

4. **Grow and/or revise the list** in the light of feedback from (3). Make sure you write these skills down and ensure they appear on your CV and at interview.

COLLECTING THE EVIDENCE

5. **Take a reality check.** Make sure you have enough evidence for each skill area.

   Try to create a list of positive examples that demonstrate your level of competence, eg raised £10,000 fundraising for Children in Need.

6. **Refine** your list if you cannot provide enough physical or verbal evidence.

7. **Keep a record** of all your positive feedback and achievements and make sure it remains up to date (it will come in really useful when you're feeling low or have just been rejected).

REVIEWING YOUR SKILLS

8. **Look at the resulting list** in (6) and think about which of these skills you would like to use a great deal in the future – these are your core portfolio of skills, ie the things you're good at and enjoy.

9. **Revisit** the skills you either haven't highlighted or do not have enough evidence of.

   Highlight those you feel are crucial to maintaining your employability in the short and medium term. These are your areas for development.

10. **Think** about whether you have the right balance of self-reliance, people, generalist and specialist skills to stay employable.

11. **Ensure** your key skills are emphasised on your CV and in interviews.

Skills portfolio (highlight any word that describes you)

PEOPLE SKILLS

Teamworking
Supportive, facilitator, organised, co-ordinator, deliverer, imaginative, delegator, open-minded

Leadership
Dynamic, motivator, team-builder, confidence booster, energetic, capable, outward-looking, accountable, visionary

Interpersonal skills
Listener, adviser, counsellor, politically aware, initiator, professional, co-operative, constructive, assertive

Customer orientation
Welcoming, friendly, caring, approachable, constructive, accommodating, tactful, diplomatic, tolerant

Oral communication
Educator, trainer, communicator, presenter, promoter, influencer, humorous, empathetic, telephone skills

Foreign language
Specific language skills, cultural awareness, international experience, written and oral expertise, sensitivity

SELF-RELIANCE SKILLS

Self-awareness /confidence
Purposeful, focused, reflective, perceptive, honest, self-belief, objective, realistic, balanced

Self-promotion skills
Positive, persuasive, pleasant, proactive, persistent, ambitious, opportunistic, promoter

Initiative and proactivity
Resourceful, energetic, drive, flexible, self-starter, self-reliant, initiative, self-disciplined

Networking skills
Initiator, trustful, personable, relationship-builder, persistent developer, resourceful, respected

Willing to learn
Motivated, adaptable, enthusiastic, active, keen learner, inquisitive, continual improver

Action planning
Decision-maker, planner, organised, negotiator, responsive, evaluator, forward thinker, target-driven, able to prioritise

GENERALIST SKILLS

Problem-solving
Achiever, successful, results-orientated, project management, creative, practical, logical, astute, agile mind

IT/computer literacy
IT skills, software packages, common sense, task-orientated, progressive, specific, office skills, keyboard skills

Flexibility
Multi-disciplinary, flexible, versatile, multi-skilled, willing, obliging, mobile, adaptable

Numeracy skills
Accurate, logical, problem-solver, detailed, methodical, consistent, quick thinker, analytical, thorough

Business acumen
Competitive, entrepreneurial, enterprising, commercial, foresight, budgeter, risk taker, effective written communication

Commitment
Dedicated, trustworthy, conscientious, reliable, loyal, punctual, knowledgeable, experienced

SPECIALIST SKILLS

Company-specific skills
Specialist knowledge, eg product or market knowledge; specialist skills, eg IT packages; unique language skills, eg Chinese; specialist interpersonal skills, eg public speaker

Technical skills
Professional, sector-based or functional skills, eg journalism, research, aerospace engineering, tax accounting, counselling, creative design, economist, personnel, sales, marketing

Understanding commercial goals of company
Specialist understanding of an organisation's goals, priorities and future direction (combination of self-reliance, business acumen and people skills)

You have more skills than you think

You'll be amazed at how many skills you possess once you start to look at yourself in a wider perspective. That means taking into account the kind of things you get involved in away from your normal full-time occupation.

The example overleaf illustrates the benefits of thinking on a broader perspective.

"I'm only a marketing/admin assistant"

Try the exercise for yourself – looking at your family, social life and other non-work-related activities.
You'll be surprised how many skills you really have...

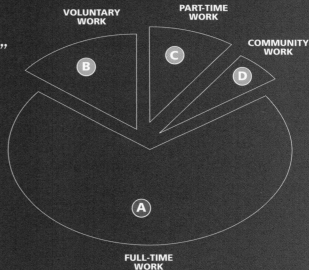

VOLUNTARY WORK

PART-TIME WORK

COMMUNITY WORK

B

C

D

A

FULL-TIME WORK

"I'm only a marketing/admin assistant"

A Full-time work - Marketing/admin assistant

TASKS / SKILLS GAINED	WORKING WITH DATA/INFORMATION	WORKING WITH PEOPLE	WORKING WITH PRACTICAL THINGS	WORKING WITH IDEAS
FILING	Administrative and organisational skills			
RECORD KEEPING	Numeracy and literacy skills			
DEALING WITH CLIENT PHONE CALLS		Listening, customer service and telephone skills		Problem-solving
OFFICE ORGANISATION	Results-driven	Using own initiative, interpersonal skills	Keyboard skills	Decision making
MARKET RESEARCH AND ANALYSIS	Evaluation, analytical report- writing, eye for detail, critical objective	Interview technique		Creative report-writing
MARKETING MAIL SHOTS AND CAMPAIGNS	Organising, planning, working under pressure	Delegating, co-ordinating, target-setting	IT skills	Marketing and creative writing skills
DATABASE DEVELOPMENT	Project management, problem-solving	Liaising with staff members	Specialist IT skills	Designing user-friendly layouts
LIAISING WITH SALES AND OTHER TEAMS		Networking, negotiation, listening, interpersonal, tact and patience		Idea generation
COMPETITION AND PRICING SURVEYS	Business acumen, financial expertise	Interviewing, telephone techniques, trustworthy		Graphic design

"I'm only a marketing/admin assistant"

B Voluntary work - leader, social club for adults with learning difficulties

TASKS / SKILLS GAINED	WORKING WITH DATA/INFORMATION	WORKING WITH PEOPLE	WORKING WITH PRACTICAL THINGS	WORKING WITH IDEAS
ORGANISING FUND RAISING EVENTS	Finance and budgeting skills	Organising, motivating, decision-making, initiating, managing, self-discipline		Creative and entrepreneurial skills
LEADING A TEAM OF HELPERS	Target-setting, performance management	Motivating, influencing, persuading, co-ordinating, teambuilding, communicating		
RUNNING NOVEL SOCIAL ACTIVITIES	Planning, organising and budgeting	Self-confidence, self-reliance, managing, coping with difficult people		Idea-generating, creativity
SUPPORTING CLUB MEMBERS AND THEIR FAMILIES		Understanding special needs, caring, listening, empathising, encouraging, challenging, liaising	Keyboard skills	Problem-solving
ATTRACTING NEW VOLUNTEERS	Researching	Promoting, selling, marketing		Resourceful, graphic design skills

"I'm only a marketing/admin assistant"

C Part-time Work - Waitress

SKILLS GAINED / TASKS	WORKING WITH DATA/INFORMATION	WORKING WITH PEOPLE	WORKING WITH PRACTICAL THINGS	WORKING WITH IDEAS
SETTING TABLES			Handling items rapidly	Thinking of new table layouts
SEATING PEOPLE. TAKING ORDERS	Explaining menu items Writing clearly to be understood by others	Customer care, listening, helping, welcoming		Providing creative options
DELIVERING ORDERS TO KITCHEN	Detailed, consistent, organised	Checking for understanding, maintaining relationships		Thinking of new systems for dealing with orders
SERVING FOOD	Ability to memorise	Flexible, quick thinker	Balancing items	
DEALING WITH CUSTOMERS	Negotiation skills	Being persuasive, listening, caring, tact, diplomacy and patience		Creative thinking
DELIVERING BILLS. TAKING MONEY AND GIVING CHANGE	Financial awareness, numeracy	Customer service, approachable, friendly	Coping under pressure	
THANKING CUSTOMERS		Dealing with people courteously		

"I'm only a marketing/admin assistant"

D Community work - running local youth hockey team

SKILLS GAINED / TASKS	WORKING WITH DATA/INFORMATION	WORKING WITH PEOPLE	WORKING WITH PRACTICAL THINGS	WORKING WITH IDEAS
TRAINING HOCKEY SKILLS			Organising training resources and equipment	Creative teaching techniques
ORGANISING MATCHES	Scheduling	Teaching, coaching, motivating		Providing creative options
ARRANGING TRANSPORT	Logistical skills, arranging finances	Liaising, listening, arranging, telephone skills	Minibus driving	
MOTIVATING THE TEAM	Reviewing performances (good and bad)	Encouraging, leading, motivating, confidence boosting, persuading		
GETTING NEW PLAYERS INTO THE TEAM		Influencing, selling, persuading, negotiation skills		Creating incentives, novel ideas
KEEPING THE TEAM RUNNING	Purchasing/organising	Delegating tasks	Helping with ground maintenance	Fundraising, enterprising

Action prompts

My skills portfolio and areas for development

Make time to map out, collect evidence of, and review your skills portfolio.

Identify the skills you really enjoy using and concentrate on three or four that make you more employable.

Then jot down notes on what you need to do. This will help you focus on the areas where you need to concentrate your efforts. Just creating the list of action prompts will also help fix it in your mind.

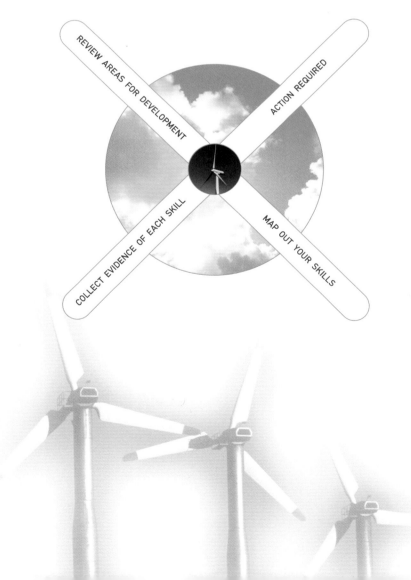

REVIEW AREAS FOR DEVELOPMENT

ACTION REQUIRED

COLLECT EVIDENCE OF EACH SKILL

MAP OUT YOUR SKILLS

finding your
ideal job

TACTIC

T2

TWO

One thing is **certain**- the **clearer** you can picture your **ideal** job, the **easier** it will be to seize it

Finding your ideal job

In this *Tactic* you will discover:

- **The word that reveals your ideal job**

- **The way to bring that job one step nearer**

***Tactic 1* should have given you a clearer idea of your skills.**

***Tactic 2* will help you decide how you can best use them. In other words it will help you define the role in life that's right for you.**

For simplicity we'll call this your ideal job. In fact it may simply be your ideal role in life, a series of jobs in a particular career area – or a project to which you devote yourself.

Remember, we're all different, and we all have our own priorities. Remember too that we change as we go through life and gain experience – and so do our ideas.

Like winning the lottery, many people just sit there waiting hopefully for this 'ideal job' to land in their lap. We can assure you it will be an extremely long wait.

There may well be such a job or role in life that is ideal for you – but it won't suddenly appear with bright flashing lights. It is more likely to come in some unexpected way.

One thing is certain. The clearer you can picture your ideal job, the easier it will be to spot and seize it when it appears.

You also need to accept that few people actually achieve the ideal. The important thing is to keep getting closer to it all the time.

KEEP IT REAL!
Cocktail tester in a tropical beach bar might sound the ideal job. But you might not have the tastebuds (or the temperament). More realistically, your ideal should be to make the most of your individual talent and motivation – usually the best recipe for long-term satisfaction.

The word that reveals your ideal job

To help you aim for what you really want, we've devised a simple method of focusing on the job or role that's right for you. It's summed up in one word: *PROCESS*.

This is both a useful acronym and exactly what it says – a process.

These seven elements sum up the key choices to make when picturing your ideal job.

These areas are closely related so don't worry too much if you duplicate some answers – it's the process that counts.

To help you think about them in more depth, you will find a fuller explanation with lots of prompts to give you ideas in *Your personal ingredients for success* (page 22).

You will then be in the best position to act by completing the profile of *Your ideal job* (page 26).

PURPOSE

Try to identify the main purpose of your ideal job/life role. How does work relate to your wider life ambitions? Does it provide your satisfaction – or simply finance other interests which give you more of a buzz. In short, do you live to work or work to live?

ROLES

What kind of work do you see yourself doing to satisfy this purpose? What suits your temperament best? Do you prefer working with people, ideas or practical things?

ORGANISATION

Do you see yourself working in the private sector or for a public body – in industry or an office? Would you feel more relaxed in a large organisation or a small private firm?

CAREER MOTIVATION

This is the big one – and it's very closely related to purpose (above). What really motivates you? Do you see yourself working for someone else – or working for yourself? A settled job, a series of roles in a particular career area – or a special project of some kind? How important is security against the need to strike out into new fields?

There are many vital issues here so be sure to *think*.

ENVIRONMENT

What energises you most – a steady pace or the stimulation of deadlines? Do you prefer dealing with ideas or working in a hands-on way? Think about the kind of work you enjoy most, the way you interact with others, the social context, the learning environment you prefer, the working relationships (and hours) you enjoy most.

SECTOR

What kind of employment sectors suit you best? – your choices might range from communications to engineering and from professional services to retail or leisure.

You also need to check if there are signs of growth in your target sector and where the main opportunities lie.

SKILLS

Finally you need to ask what key skills, qualifications and experience you need for your ideal job – remember to look at it from the employer's perspective. Try a 'gap analysis' to see how the portfolio of skills you have identified in **Tactic 1** compares with what you really need.

Bringing that ideal job closer

First time round, you may have a very blurred or unrealistic picture of your ideal job. You can make things clearer by:

- Continually **revisiting the PROCESS** either by yourself or with a friend or colleague asking you the questions.

- **Sending off** for as many different **job specifications** as possible. Highlight the requirements you would meet and enjoy. You will then have a bank of activities which interest you.

- **Creating** as many different **opportunities** as possible to find and test out your ideal job.

- **Looking at the stepping stones** that will get you there, eg voluntary work, temporary work or a particular project

- **Discarding** the kind of roles you hate

- **Following your instincts** – and looking for clues in your past

It's important to accept that this is a learning process. We all find out new things about ourselves over the years – and the following pages will help you understand the **PROCESS**.

YOUR KEY TASK
The more research work you do and the more experience you gain, the more focused your ideas will be. Your key task is to move from 'I think I know what I want' to 'I know what I want' to 'I've got what I want.'

STEVE'S STORY

Steve expects everything on a plate. He saw his ideal job as a media journalist but had no writing experience or self-reliance skills. Two years later, assuming the world owes him a living, he is still going nowhere fast.

Yet with a more practical and realistic approach – and persistence – he could still move along his chosen career path.

AND REMEMBER...
you may not have to leave your current position to find your ideal job – you may simply need to reshape your role. You may find the key to achieving this lies in project work, voluntary work or simply trying a new experience.

Your personal ingredients for success

This exercise will help you think about the various ingredients that go to make up your ideal job.
The more you go through the *PROCESS* and think about these elements, the clearer your picture will be –
and the easier you'll find it when you later start trying to spot hidden opportunities.

PURPOSE
– what is the main purpose of your ideal job?

Don't get hung up on job titles. Can you look beyond broad job titles such as marketing and personnel and identify the purpose in more detail? Think about how you see the main outcomes of your work and ask yourself what you hope to achieve and how this fits in to your broader goals.

ROLES
– of your ideal job

Can you identify the five main tasks or responsibilities in your ideal job? Do you prefer working with detail, ideas, people, or practical things? What roles give you a real buzz? What percentage of your time would you prefer to be:

Managing	◯ %
Communicating	◯ %
Innovating	◯ %
Promoting	◯ %
Developing	◯ %
Organising	◯ %
Producing	◯ %
Inspecting	◯ %
Maintaining	◯ %
Advising	◯ %

What roles do you and other people think you're good at?

ORGANISATION
– what type of organisation would you ideally like to work in?

◯ Voluntary/non-profit-making

◯ Community-based

◯ Public sector

◯ Commercial

◯ Industrial

◯ Manufacturing

◯ Service

◯ Multinational

– what culture?

It is vital to find the right kind of culture for you. You need to target the kind of firm that will allow you to feel comfortable and confident at work. This will depend on such factors as:

- Style of management

- Company values

- Norms and expectations

- Performance measurement methods

- Family-friendly policies

– what size?

◯ Small (1 – 49 employees)

◯ Medium (50 – 249)

◯ Large (over 250)

It's worth looking at the pros and cons of working in a large or small organisation.

Small organisation

POTENTIAL ADVANTAGES

- Early responsibility
- Chance to make significant impact
- Variety and challenge
- Positive role models
- Forced to become extremely self-reliant
- Growth in new job opportunities

RISKS

- Lack of structured support and training
- A different kind of career progression (fewer layers of management offering promotion)
- Potential insecurity, short-term contracts
- Low public image of small businesses but everybody knows big, blue chip companies
- Potentially fewer people to meet

Large organisation

POTENTIAL ADVANTAGES

- Structured training and development opportunities
- Clearer career progression
- Ready-made support networks
- Competitive salary
- Potentially higher level of security
- Higher public awareness and credibility

RISKS

- Small cog in large wheel
- Lower levels of overall influence and impact on the business
- Less immediate task variety
- Potential to get stuck in a rut
- More impersonal
- Higher chances of being underemployed

CAREER MOTIVATION
– what drives you?

We can be motivated by different things at different stages of our lives. You should regularly review the list on the following page.

1. Ask yourself how important each of the following statements is in your future job.

2. Tick an appropriate box for each statement, only using the 'absolutely essential' box when you simply cannot do without it.

3. Add to the list any other personally important statements.

4. Revisit the list and think honestly:

   How realistic is it to achieve all the 'absolutely essential' and 'very important' statements?

   Do any compromises have to be made? Eg if you don't want to move geographically, it will be hard to build a multinational business.

5. Keep a record of your finalised 'absolutely essential' statements and assess the extent to which your current or future position meets these.

What do you want from a job? Example: I think freedom to make my own decisions is important in my future job (shown below ✓)

	ABSOLUTELY ESSENTIAL	VERY IMPORTANT	IMPORTANT	FAIRLY IMPORTANT	NOT IMPORTANT
AUTONOMY					
Freedom to make my own decisions			✓		
Working autonomously					
Freedom from organisational rules and constraints					
Ability to define my own tasks, schedules and procedures					
Pursuing an independent career on my terms					
STABILITY & SECURITY					
A clearly mapped-out career path					
Job that requires steady, predictable performance					
Long-term security and stability					
Working in a stable, well-known organisation					
Incremental pay and benefits based on length of service					
ENTERPRISE					
Creating new organisations, products and services					
Building my own business					
Owning something developed from my ideas and efforts					
Producing things that people associate with me					
Showing people I can build a fortune					
SENSE OF PURPOSE					
Providing a service to help others					
Contributing to the wider community					
Dedication to a particular course					
Having a job of real value					
Making a difference in the world					
BALANCED LIFESTYLE					
A balanced personal and professional lifestyle					
Flexible working hours and practices (able to work at home)					
Work that minimises interference with personal/family life					
Relatively low levels of geographical movement					
Sufficient time for pastimes, holidays and relaxing					
EXPERTISE & CHALLENGE					
Developing a specialism to a high level of excellence					
Being recognised as an expert in the field					
Ability to use my special skills and talents					
Solving complex problems					
Regular challenges to stretch my abilities and skills					
REWARD & RECOGNITION					
Having a high standard of living					
Being recognised for my achievements					
Having a highly paid job					
Being highly regarded by others					
Reaching a respected social status					
AUTHORITY & INFLUENCE					
Responsibility for making major decisions					
Advancement up the organisational ladder					
Ability to influence, supervise, lead and control people					
Contributing to the success of my organisation					
Accountability for finances and resources					

ENVIRONMENT
– what type of working environment energises you?

○ Pressurised
○ Challenging
○ Working outdoors
○ Unstressed atmosphere
○ Steady routine
○ Office-based
○ Home-based
○ Analytical
○ Well-structured
○ Independent
○ Project-based
○ Working with people
○ Ideas/creativity
○ Autonomy/freedom
○ Team-orientated
○ Practical/hands-on
○ Working with data/information/detail
○ Geographic mobility

– if you want to work with people, in what way?

○ Visiting, dealing, liaising
○ Teaching, educating, promoting
○ Advising, servicing, problem-solving
○ Managing, motivating, co-ordinating
○ Disciplining, organising, controlling
○ Other combination

… in what context?

○ Social
○ Business
○ Education
○ Community

… and with what age group/personality/ability?

– what type of learning environment do you work best in?

○ Active – chance to get actively involved
○ Reflective – time and opportunity to sit back and think things through
○ Pragmatic – chance to work practically with things
○ Theoretical – opportunities to look at underlying principles and concepts

What type of working relationships do you enjoy – relaxed, formal, informal, autonomous, team-based, professional, pressurised…

What kind of working hours? 9 – 5, flexible, part-time?

What other characteristics are important?

SECTOR
– can you identify one or two ideal sectors to work in?

Here are just a few examples:

Employment sectors

Hospitality management	Construction
Transport/travel	Retail/wholesale
Communications	Health
IT/computers/ telecommunications	Environment
Manufacturing/recycling	Media/marketing/PR
Engineering	Sports/entertainment
Public/government	Financial
Professional services	Legal
Utilities	Voluntary/charity
Education/training	Pharmaceuticals/ chemicals/processing
Agriculture and land management	Food
Arts/culture	Consumer goods
Tourism/leisure	Elderly care
Technological/scientific	

Are there signs of growth in your target sector (eg, job announcements, economic forecasts, consumer demand, share prices, new contracts, companies moving into the area, new technological developments, your own intuition etc)?

Which are the key organisations?

Where do the main opportunities lie?

Do they require the types of skills you have?

Do they offer the experience you need?

SKILLS
– what key skills, qualifications and experience are required to perform effectively in your ideal job?

• Put yourself in the shoes of a recruiter. Analyse the objectives, roles, tasks etc and identify the criteria for a successful candidate. List the skills, qualifications and experience required

• Compare this list with your current portfolio of skills (see **Tactic 1**)

• Identify the major gaps. Eg I need more fundraising experience

Action prompts

Your ideal job

Use the following key headings to draw up a profile of your ideal job.

When noting down your prompts, refer to the detailed _PROCESS_ pages to help you _think_ more deeply about your answers.

Identify the actions needed to get you one step nearer to your ideal job

PROCESS

PURPOSE
how does your work relate to your life?

ROLE
what type of work?

ORGANISATION
type/size?

CAREER MOTIVATION
important characteristics/benefits

ENVIRONMENT
physical/social/learning

SECTOR
type

SKILLS
key skills/qualifications and experience required

revealing the secret jobs market

TACTIC

T3

THREE

The **harder** I work
the **luckier** I get

Revealing the secret jobs market

In this *Tactic* you will discover:

- **20 ways to uncover hidden opportunities**

- **How to make a career reality check**

People's careers are rarely built on the jobs they want to do most.

All too often their career is shaped by chance – it just depends on the jobs they fall into first.

As we've seen, many people spend at least 40 years of 40 weeks and 40 hours a week in employment – yet still devote more time to planning their holiday than their career.

If you are willing to invest a little time now in creatively exploring your options, you'll be paid back ten times over in future career satisfaction. But where do you start exploring?

Naturally you need to do the usual things such as scanning the 'Jobs vacant' adverts and checking with careers services and JobCentres. For a quick refresher go to *Don't forget the visible jobs market* (page 31).

But today, the real opportunities are less likely than ever to be signposted with flashing lights – a mere 20% of job vacancies are advertised through traditional media such as local and national press.

That's why you need to discover the hidden jobs market.

Just like the proverbial iceberg, 80% of the vast mass of opportunities are buried out of sight, many within little-known small businesses.

All too many people are unaware of this invisible – but highly rewarding – source of opportunities. And because most people are simply reactive to the traditional job adverts, they end up competing in an already overcrowded marketplace.

The key to success is to be proactive and uncover this little-known market. This may require some craftiness, effort and persistence. It will sometimes mean looking beyond your own cosy comfort zone.

But it has to be worth investing a few days or weeks of your time and energy to avoid being condemned to a lifetime in a job you hate.

How do you tap into this hidden jobs market? There are many, many ways – and it may need only one of them to get you moving.

You'll be amazed how many opportunities you can unearth by a spot of action research. For example, digging around in your neighbourhood can be surprisingly productive. You could try:

- **checking** on news about firms in the local paper

- **strolling** round a nearby business park

- **offering** your services as a freelance worker or volunteer

- **chatting** to local people

Any of these activities could throw up a vital opening or produce a rewarding lead. And if you pay attention to timing – seizing an opportunity as it occurs or meeting an employer's urgent need, it's amazing how successful you can be.

This is merely one approach – overleaf, you'll find a whole ideas bank to help you think in *20 top tips to reveal hidden opportunities.*

Dip into these whenever you're looking for new ways to move your career along.

Try also to look beyond your existing horizon and focus on your longer-term expectations.

Think about the suggestions in *Looking ahead* (page 31).

In the meantime you need to *act* by carrying out the specific tasks in the *Action Prompts*.

- Uncovering the opportunities – will give you a practical plan for applying some of those 20 top tips.

- Making a reality check – asks you to revisit the ideal job you defined in **Tactic 2** in the light of the experience gained when you put some of those tips into action.

IT'S UP TO YOU!
What you put in is what you get out.
And today this is truer than ever.
For in the new world of work
there are far more opportunities
than ever before.

TRY THIS NOW!
Creating your own opportunities
is an ongoing process. You can put
these ideas into action all the time.
So use them to grow your own job
– and not only when you're
looking for a new one.

20 top tips to reveal
hidden opportunities

1. Be positive and realistic. Dedicate time to the process and recognise it's a long-term investment. Develop key skills such as telephone technique, high-level research and networking skills, perseverance and an acceptance of rejection. Accept rejection as a part of the process.

2. List your existing network of contacts – family, friends, neighbours, colleagues, past lecturers, present and past employers. Find out what careers they're in and how they can help in your job search and if they know anybody else who can help. Ask people for an advisory interview (see Tactic 6).

3. Be prepared to take a few stepping stones to your ideal job. You may need to take a temporary or lower-grade job to create the right networks. Remember it's easier to get a job when you're in one already.

4. Identify two or three people working in your chosen field and seek an advisory interview. Ask how to research the market, who to speak to, where to find information and what questions to ask. Keep them informed of your progress.

5. Get as many people as possible looking for you.
Sign up with a recruitment agency, let previous employers and current contacts know you're available and send out speculative letters.

6. Identify one or two sectors in which you would ideally like to work (hopefully growing ones) and do market research. Look beyond the big names to their suppliers, distributors, customers and competitors. In particular, look at the small businesses growing within these sectors.

7. Scan your local paper for signs of growth, eg companies that are expanding, new developments, government tenders and awards. Make contact before new jobs are advertised.

8. Keep in touch with changes in your chosen field by reviewing journals, trade magazines, newsletters, electronic media – databases, teletext, internet, CD Roms and attending conferences and trade fairs. The information section librarian can prove an invaluable ally.

9. Look for work-shadowing opportunities.
Find out whether companies have open days/visits. Look at where they promote their products or services. Use careers fairs and employer presentations to find out what job roles involve.

10. Pinpoint three or four professional or trade journals. Contact authors of any interesting articles for an advisory interview. Also look for companies appointing staff – it may indicate expansion (but regular ads may mean high staff turnover!)

11. Find a forum for meeting new people who can help your job search, eg join a professional association; volunteer for community, civic or professional projects and extend your social network. Tap into new networks.

12. Always do your groundwork before sending off speculative letters. Know who you're targeting, what you're asking for, develop a persuasive covering letter and follow up with a phone call. Be persistent and play the percentage game.

13. Volunteer to work unpaid or on a trial basis (particularly useful in small businesses which see recruiting new staff as risky). Use any opportunity (eg a specific project) to show your abilities – and make sure your client spreads the word to colleagues and their networks.

14. Get on the inside track by keeping in touch with people in your chosen field/organisation. Tap into their information networks, eg internal vacancy lists, newsletters, press announcements etc.

15. Draw up a hit list of organisations to target.
Get names from Yellow Pages, trade association directories, professional journals, Chambers of Commerce, National Training Organisations (NTOs), local business associations, Business Links and Government Training Organisations. Make a speculative application or give them a phone call.

USE YOUR CONTACTS!
You'll find it much easier to look ahead and improve your focus if you take the trouble to build a good network.

toptipstoptipstoptipstoptipstoptipstoptipstoptipstoptips

Don't forget the visible jobs market

As well as being proactive, it's vital to ensure you make the most of traditional options.

Some key tips include:

- **Find out** which days your local and national newspapers advertise particular kinds of jobs

- **Don't be put off** by job titles and salaries – scan job adverts in detail to find out exactly what they entail. If in doubt, ask for more information

- **Approach your local careers service** (private or local university) or JobCentre. Make specific contacts and develop relationships with staff who may be able to help you in your job search. If they can't help you, ask them who can

- **Get yourself onto** as many useful **mailing lists** as possible

- **Keep up to date** with the directories, publications, journals and magazines through which employers recruit, and make sure you surf the **internet**

- **Investigate** a possible personal or career development course

16 **Advertise yourself** – eg write articles for the local press, business magazines, professional journals, the internet, or promote yourself at trade fairs – anywhere businesses may look.
Keep your CV up to date and adapted for different jobs. Offer your services as a consultant or freelance. If you can't get a job, get a client. This year, you may only have one client, next year two... and so on.

17 **Enrol in a class or join a network** related to your field/industry. You'll not only learn new things but also build new contacts. Try to link into different types of networks.

18 **Catch opportunities before they go public.**
New contracts, people retiring or leaving their jobs, market changes, new regulations, company relocation, entry into new markets and increasing share prices are all signs of potential new jobs.

19 **Get yourself out and about.** Walk or drive round your local business park, office complex or your local environment. Check all the business opportunities on your doorstep. Pick up any relevant information (promotional literature, brochures, chat to receptionist etc) and use this to make a speculative phone call or application.

20 **Learn from experience** – your own and other people's. Seek as much feedback as possible in order to improve your technique. Buy a book on creative thinking or innovative job search techniques. Make the most of traditional options.

Remember that thousands of people complain about rejection – but it's usually an excuse to avoid making the effort to try the ideas we've been looking at.

Most people want things on a plate. Make up your mind to be different and show initiative.

Never forget that creating your own opportunities is an ongoing process. You can also be using these ideas all the time to grow your own job – not just when you're looking for a new one.

Looking ahead

It's useful to improve your job focus by looking ahead. Try imagining you're up in the air and trying to glimpse your destination in the distance.

You could:

- **Scan the papers** and cut out job advertisements that would really appeal to you in three to five years time. Keep a scrapbook.

- **Put yourself in the shoes of employers** recruiting for these positions. What skills and experiences are they looking for? Now look at where you are now (see **Tactic 1**) and what new experience you require.

- **Ask friends and colleagues** what they see you achieving in career terms.
This may open up new options you haven't thought of

- **Think of people** whose jobs or lifestyles you really admire and discover how they've managed their careers

- You may also wish to **investigate** psychological testing

Action prompts

UNCOVERING THE OPPORTUNITIES

1 Find out how proactive you are.

Use *The Top 20 tips to reveal hidden opportunities* to score your current performance. Score each tip from 0 (non-existent) to 5 (excellent). Maximum score 100.

Your score gives your percentage likelihood of finding your ideal job or role in life.

2 Select the three or four tips that appeal most.

Jot down daily, weekly or monthly objectives to put these ideas into action.

3 Review progress regularly and keep notes.

Don't worry if things don't initially go as planned. In the long term, the effort could prove useful in surprising ways.

MAKING A REALITY CHECK

Having explored a number of options, revisit your 'ideal job' (**Tactic 2**).

Draw up a list of action prompts by answering the following questions:

Clarify position: Does such a job/role exist? What is it – can I define the **PROCESS** (purpose, role, organisation, career motivation, environment, sector, and skills)?

Highlight gaps: What new skills, qualifications, experience do I need to achieve or grow into my ideal job? How realistic is it and what do I need to do (learn on the job, invest in a course, find a new project)? What timescale?

Identify options: What priority actions do I need to take? Are there any 'stepping stones' (opportunities, experiences, roles or positions) I need to construct? Do I know anybody who can help?

Assess compromises: What are the benefits/limitations of this career path? Do any compromises need to be made? Are the pay levels sufficient?

TAKE IT EASY!
If all this seems daunting, try to sit down with somebody and break the task into small chunks. Try also to *think* more creatively. For instance, even bucket and spade producers need marketing, financial and personnel expertise. Today, manufacturing a tea bag can demand as much technological expertise as making a mobile phone!

the
simple formula
for **selling**
yourself

TACTIC
T4
FOUR

Seeing **everybody** as a client, not an employer, and **promoting** the benefits you can bring to them are probably the **most** important qualities in life.

The simple formula for selling yourself

In this *Tactic* you will find out:

- **How to look at yourself through the client's eyes**

- **How to sell yourself on paper – and in person**

In **Tactic 3** you learned how to tap into the hidden jobs market. But once you've located a likely job or opportunity, you need to persuade someone that you're the right person for it. In other words, you need to sell yourself. And there's a simple formula for success:

Identify what your client is looking for – and how you can provide it.

We've said that managing your own career means thinking differently.

Here it means taking a completely fresh look at yourself. Not just through your own eyes – but also through those of your prospective employer.

This will help you understand the value you can bring to your clients while keeping an eye on your own values and long-term goals.

The process simply involves matching what your clients need to what you can offer (and vice versa).

In theory it looks simple. In practice too many people fail to consider what their clients need. As a result they fail to balance both sides of the equation.

This usually leads them to promote themselves in a hit-or-miss manner that rarely succeeds. They fire off thousands of bland applications, hoping one will hit the target. Or simply keep praying that one day they will stumble on a solution.

Focusing on what the client needs calls for a far more structured approach.

The previous **Tactics** in the book have already positioned you to provide this.

Tactic 1 showed you what you can do. **Tactic 2** helped you relate those skills to your ideal job and **Tactic 3** revealed some hidden opportunities.

Now you have the information and focus you need to start targeting opportunities with some accuracy. And to seize those opportunities, you need to master the practical techniques that can help you sell yourself – whether through your CV, in person or at an interview.

keeping the equation balanced

YOU OFFER

- Solution to a business need

- Specific skills, personality, attitude, knowledge and experience related to the position

- Commitment, flexibility and a willingness to learn

- Added value to the business

YOU NEED

- Your ideal job (or stepping stone to)

- Your career aims, values and motivations met

- An opportunity to learn

- Added benefits (salary, training etc)

YOUR CLIENTS NEED

- Solution to a business need

- Their job specification met

- Their personal specification met

- Someone with the right attitude, personality and commitment who is willing to learn

YOUR CLIENTS OFFER

- Experience

- Opportunity to learn

- Career development

- Benefits package (salary, pension programme, support network etc)

Selling yourself on paper—your CV

The chief way you sell yourself on paper is your CV.

We're assuming you already have a CV in some form.
You may have used one of the 101 books on how to write a CV,
copied a friend's format or asked someone to advise you.

This **Tactic** will ask you to *act* by updating your existing CV

You should *think* about this by using *Creating a CV that sells*
(page 38).

There is no such thing as a perfect CV. Its chances of success
or failure depend completely on how far it meets the criteria,
background and bias of the person reading it –
your prospective client.

**That's why you will also need to adapt your CV to every
client you approach. It will then be focused on meeting
their needs – not yours!**

Taking a client-centred approach to self-promotion will help
maximise your chances of success, whatever your situation.
Don't forget to keep reviewing and improving your CV. Like all
career development, it needs to be a dynamic, ongoing process.

**KEEP YOUR
CV TO HAND!**
Your CV needs to encapsulate
your up-to-date portfolio of skills
and experience. It must capture you
as a living and breathing person.
And that means keeping it handy
and up to date – not gathering
dust in the back of a drawer.

Selling yourself in person

**Did you realise you are being interviewed each day?
whenever you make a phone call, stop for a chat or
work with a colleague, people are forming opinions
of your skills.**

All the time you have opportunities to build relationships and
subtly sell your skills and qualities to the people around you.
When you make a presentation, a speech or participate in a
conference or seminar, you are raising your profile even higher.

Yet marketing or selling ourselves rarely comes naturally.
Learning to sell yourself is a critical skill and needs developing
over time – so use every opportunity for practice.
Think about this, using *10 top tips to communicate better*
(page 40).

Selling yourself at interviews

Everything you learn about selling yourself in person will pay off when it comes to interviews. But there are also special skills you can develop to boost your performance.

You also need to ensure you're thoroughly prepared and organised every time you go for an interview. – *Your interview checklist* (page 41).

Perhaps the most important thing is to understand what lies behind a line of questioning. Again, that involves looking through the eyes of the interviewer or employer. To help you think about this, use *The 20 toughest questions you'll ever be asked* (page 42).

Keeping your ego in shape

There's nothing more certain in a successful career than being rejected loads of times – we can assure you of that from personal experience. And that's why self-confidence is one of the keys to success.

Regular helpings of self-confidence can:

- Improve your **self-image**

- Help you **deal with rejection** in a positive light

- Enable you to **cope** with unforeseen circumstances

- Encourage others to **believe** in you and your abilities.

Yet believe it or not, it's easier than you might think to boost your self-esteem and self-confidence. All you need do is follow a few simple rules.

To *think* about this, use *Your 10 top morale boosters* (page 44).

REMEMBER
CVs, other documents and interviews are not the only opportunities to sell yourself. Everything you say and do in your day-to-day business life can be an opportunity for self-promotion.

Creating a CV that sells

Use this checklist every time you update your CV or send a copy to a prospective employer.

Remember to tick every box honestly and you will have a CV that correctly meets the needs of your client – rather than your own!

A. IDENTIFY YOUR CUSTOMER NEEDS

Step 1 – Put yourself in the employer's shoes

◯ Have you dissected the job advert and specification and done your research?

◯ Have you written a clear list of the skills, qualities and experience essential for the position? Can you back it up with evidence?

◯ Are you using the right language? (Key words can often be found in a company's brochure, website or publicity material).

◯ Have you spoken directly (phone or in person) to anyone about the opportunity? This is rarely done, but gives you three invaluable assets:

- Unique information on what exactly is required

- Evidence that you are proactive and motivated to bother finding out more

- A more personal, customised approach to your covering letter

◯ Do you know anybody who works for the organisation (or in another organisation) with whom you could discuss the opportunity?

◯ Have you contacted them for advice?

Step 2 – Understand the market needs

◯ Your CV needs to be fully market-tested.

◯ Have you looked at what employers in your field expect?

◯ Have you sought expert feedback on your draft CV from colleagues, specialists and careers experts?

◯ Do you adapt your CV to each job you apply for?

◯ Have you looked at other people's CVs so you can improve yours?

◯ Have you found a good book on how to write a CV?

◯ Have you assessed different styles and layouts?

◯ Do you realise you'll receive conflicting advice and need to use your own judgement?

B. MATCH YOURSELF TO THESE NEEDS

Step 3 – Sell the benefits you can offer

◯ Don't give employers long descriptions – just a summary of your skills, experiences and achievements and how they can benefit their organisation.

◯ Are you clear on which of your qualities are vital for this position (link Step 1 above with your skills portfolio in **Tactic 1** of this book)

◯ Are you clear on what makes you stand out from the competition (your unique selling points)?

◯ Have you clearly stated how your benefits and skills are relevant to the job?

◯ Are you using action words?

◯ Are you using the appropriate style and language for your chosen profession? This can only be assessed by testing your CV out with people in the field or reviewing successful CVs.

Step 4 – Make your CV employer-friendly

◯ You need to make it as easy as possible for the employer to say yes.

◯ Are the selection criteria clearly met?

◯ Have you positioned your key messages for maximum impact on the page (eg top and bottom).

◯ Have you included the following:

- **Career profile** – summarizing key skills, experience and suitability for the job in a 3-4 line personal profile

- **Work experience** – listing most relevant and recent experience first, highlighting achievements, roles and responsibilities

- **Qualifications** – Most relevant and up to date first

- **Key skills** – List evidence of key skills for the job

- **Specialist skills** – Highlight unique skills and experience

- **Personal and professional development** – Provide evidence of your willingness to learn

- **Personal details** – Short and to the point

- **References** – Relevant to the job

And don't waffle!

Step 5 – Provide relevant evidence

○ Is there enough in-depth evidence to make you stand out? (We've all been a prefect or in a sports team, but have you co-ordinated an event, chaired a group or led a successful initiative?)

○ Have you highlighted voluntary or other unique work? This is strong evidence of character and motivation.

○ Are you providing the right balance of evidence? (You may need to juggle sections around for different jobs)

○ Are you being honest? Can all statements be backed up at interview? Can you deliver everything you promise?

○ Does the evidence persuade the recruiter that you can do the job in the future?

Step 6 – Go for lively, logical layout

○ Does your CV make the employer instantly pick it out?

○ Is the information clear and well presented within two pages?

○ Does the sequence of sections work in your favour, with the most interesting stuff first and last?

○ Is there a sense of a living, breathing person behind the words and format?

○ Does your CV stand out from the crowd? Is the appearance professional (perfectly word-processed, good-quality paper, easy-to-read layout, and only two pages)?

○ Have you cut out all padding, negativity and irrelevant information?

Step 7 – Show commitment, focus and enthusiasm

○ This might sound hard on paper. But good planning and a carefully worded covering letter will put the message across.

○ Have you contacted the organisation to find out more (and promote yourself informally)?

○ Have you used your network to gain additional information?

○ Does your covering letter:

- Customise and personalise your application (addressing a targeted individual)

- Clarify your motivation for the job?

- Demonstrate that you have a clear knowledge of what it entails?

- Summarise the key skills and experiences that match you to the job?

- Provide any vital information missing from the CV?

- Bring your CV to life?

- End on a positive, forward-looking note?

C. SEEK FEEDBACK

Step 8 – Continually seek feedback and improve

○ The quality of your CV will improve the more times you go through this process. Have you:

- Gained constructive feedback from experts in the field?

- Asked the views of a couple of friends?

- Gained constructive feedback from a careers specialist?

- Taken on board the feedback?

- Trained yourself to keep reviewing the changing needs of employers and adapt your CV to respond?

- Remembered to keep updating your CV, identifying gaps and adding new skills, qualities and experience?

Step 9 – Deal positively with rejection

○ Have you gained any feedback following a rejection? (Don't just accept they're too busy without even trying).

○ Do you realise that rejection may be nothing to do with your personal qualities (eg internal candidate, wrong company, job below your abilities)?

○ Can you revisit this checklist each time you receive a rejection?

○ Do you need to make any improvements?

○ Do you look at rejection positively – ie they're the ones losing out.

○ Are you being realistic and persistent enough? Eight rejections out of ten may seem negative. But that creates two positive 'hits'

Step 10 – Recognise your successes

Your successes can be just as revealing as your failures. And they provide an opportunity to lay the foundations for further success. Once you understand what you are doing right, you are in a position to repeat it. And again, remember to look at yourself from the employer's viewpoint.

toptipstoptipstoptipstoptipstoptipstoptipstoptipstoptipstoptipstoptips

10 top tips to communicate better

Marketing or selling ourselves rarely comes naturally. Self-promotion is a critical skill that needs developing over time – so use every opportunity to build these skills. Here are a few ideas for action:

1. **Take a course** in communication skills and understand the fundamentals of effective presentation. Make presentations yourself – and study other people's.
2. **Volunteer** for as many presentations as possible – aim for at least two major ones a year.
3. **Plan** carefully and understand its importance, eg for anticipating an audience's needs, objective-setting, developing a clear structure, rehearsing awkward questions etc.
4. **Get involved** in the community and learn to communicate with other cultural and educational groups.
5. **Join a club** or society where you will promote your ideas or lead a group. Try presenting to different audiences, eg organise a quiz.
6. **Choose projects** that involve elements of oral communication.
7. **Learn** from your peers, assess the qualities of good and bad communications.
8. **Present** every project you undertake to your colleagues, your boss, your boss's boss.
9. **Seek feedback,** keep a log of your progress and even get yourself videoed to analyse your good and bad habits. Remember that everybody has disastrous presentations, so don't worry – you learn most from your flops.
10. **Don't forget** – whatever your role – practice makes perfect.

The more shy and reserved you are, the more difficult it will be to speak to large numbers of people. And you're likely to need these skills in the future as more interviews are demanding formal presentations.

Start now – if only in a small way – and gain self-confidence for later career moves.

Your interview checklist

Check through these vital dos and don'ts well in advance every time you go for an interview – it will ensure you are completely focused and in command on the big day.

DO

Research into the organisation beforehand

Act and appear professional from the first minute – first impressions count

Adapt your skills as closely to the company's needs as possible

Sell achievements and benefits you can bring

Keep positive, friendly, polite and confident and project your enthusiasm for the job

Listen to why the question is being asked

Bring support information and a list of key questions to ask

Ask questions that show you've done your background homework

Seek feedback on your performance and keep doors open if unsuccessful

DON'T

Arrive unprepared at the interview

Act too laid back and personal, although the odd bit of humour always helps

Waffle, wander or focus on your needs at the expense of the company's

Appear too cocky, undersell yourself, talk too quickly or mumble

Look unmotivated and bored

Jump in before the question has been completed

Undersell yourself by not providing back-up information

Forget to ask some positive questions yourself – it's a two-way process

Take rejection personally and end on a sour note

Make sure you review the list before – and after – every interview.

IMPROVING YOUR INTERVIEW SKILLS

Confidence is one of the secrets of a successful interview and these additional tips will help ensure you are never at a loss in those nerve-racking situations.

1. **List** all the potential questions you may be asked.

2. **Refer** back to your skills and attributes highlighted in **Tactic 1.** Update the list regularly.

3. **Seek a mock interview** from a friend or colleague using the list generated in question 1.

4. **Listen carefully** to any feedback from your mock or real interviews.

5. **Evaluate** your performance and compare your view with employers' responses.

   Learn from each experience – particularly if you are rejected.

The 20 toughest questions

This list will help give you that vital edge in interviews.

The trick, once again, is finding out what your client is looking for. Once you feel you know this, your confidence will grow.

Below is a list of questions employers often ask (including some nightmare ones). After each question we explain what information the interviewer is really looking for.

Remember to put yourself in the employer's shoes and think about what lies behind each line of questioning.

'Tell me about yourself'

Employers are looking for a quick snapshot of you (both your background and your personality) and how well you sell yourself and your capabilities. Don't ramble on.

'Why did you apply for the job?'

This looks at your levels of motivation and commitment. Make sure you research thoroughly what the job entails. State the benefits you feel you will gain and reinforce the benefits you can offer. Say why you want this job – not why you are leaving your present one.

'Tell me what you do in your spare time?'

This has a double purpose. To make sure that you have a fully-rounded personality – and ensure your hobbies won't interfere with your job. Go over your outside interests quickly, highlighting any job relevance and outlining the skills you have developed through them.

'When have you been involved in teams?'

Employers want a team player – so give examples of your role within teams (eg, creative, promoter, developer, organiser, producer, inspector, maintainer, adviser).

Underline what you learned and how it has made you more effective in a team. Link your answers directly to the job you're after – check if they're looking for a creative, resourceful team member, a detail-orientated person who will see tasks through or a positive team leader.

'What are your main strengths and weaknesses?'

This revolves around self-awareness. Again, link your strengths to the particular job. Employers want someone who knows what they are good at and where they need to improve. Everybody has weaknesses but employers want to know what you are doing to improve. Choose positive weaknesses and turn them into strengths, eg 'I'm a bit of a perfectionist, – but that's good for quality'. 'My financial skills aren't as sharp as I'd like – but I'm attending a bookkeeping night class'.

'Why should we employ you?'

What skills could add value to the company? Make brief but telling comparisons between the job description and your ability to meet their needs. State briefly what you can offer and back up anything you say with facts.

'What has been your biggest achievement?'

This reveals what motivates you and what matters to you (family, work, education or leisure?) Choose something that makes you stand out and involves positive characteristics, eg you developed determination, strength of character.

'What have you learned from your past work experiences?'

This focuses on skills developed in previous jobs (vacation, part-time, full-time). Think about those jobs. Did you have any responsibility? Pull out the positive elements and focus on benefits to the employer.

'When did you last work under pressure or deal with conflict – and how did you cope?'

This is aimed at discovering if you can deal with problems quickly and efficiently – and confront a situation if you become frustrated.

The best technique is to think of an example and explain how the situation arose – then say how you dealt with it. If asked directly if anything made you annoyed or frustrated, be truthful but avoid appearing negative.

'What is the biggest problem/dilemma you have ever faced?'

Try to choose something that will show you in a positive light. How did you get over it? What did you learn? This will not only show how you cope under stress but also your decision-making ability and strength of character.

you'll ever be asked...

'What other career opportunities are you looking at?'

This will illustrate how well you have researched and thought through your chosen career area. It will also show an employer how much you really want the job. If you just list a long series of unrelated career options, it will cast doubt on your motivation.

'Where would you like to be in five or ten years time?'

Again, if you have a clear idea, it will show your commitment and vision. If you do have some insight into where you are heading, think of some of the functions and responsibilities you would hope to have.

'When have you had to ....?'

Employers want real-life evidence that clearly demonstrates you have particular skills. Draw up a list of key skills required for the position (found by dissecting the job ad, job description and personal specification) and highlight at least two situations or achievements that prove you have each skill. Practise talking through each example and present a concise, hard-hitting case.
Avoid waffle and keep it sharp.

'What would you do in .... situation?'

Situational questions are used to test your overall style and approach. Carefully prepare by listing all the roles you'll potentially undertake in the new position and think up awkward questions yourself.

'So sell me this product.'

Role-play questions really make you think on your feet.
Once again, do your homework.
Be prepared to demonstrate your skills in action.

'What salary do you expect?'

Work out a salary range you consider reasonable –
job ads in the national and local press will give you an idea. Don't undersell (or oversell) yourself. Give a range to indicate you're prepared to negotiate.

'How competent are you at.......?'

Many employers now like to assess candidates using scoring grids with a work-based framework. This makes it important to quote practical examples showing your level of competence.

'Are you pregnant/gay/etc?'

Yes it's an outrageous question – but always be on the alert for it. It may be designed to shock you and assess your reactions. It may equally reflect the fact that some employers lack formal training in interview techniques and fall back on crude stereotypes. Whatever the reason, it's vital not to lose your cool – just write it off to ignorance.

'You haven't been much of a success so far, have you?'

The aggressive approach may also throw you. The reasons could be the same but this time it is more likely to be a deliberate attempt to unnerve you. Again, keep your composure – it's probably the reaction they are looking for.

'Do you have any questions?'

Always expect this one – so prepare a list. Include a few probing questions to show you've done your research. Don't be afraid to write them down and take them to the interview with you.

When to talk about salary?

Use your judgement here – never bring the subject up too soon. Your main priority is to promote yourself as the most suitable candidate in order to place you in a strong negotiating position. But be clear in your mind what you really want in terms of money as well as experience.

Seeking feedback

At the end of the interview seek permission (in a positive way) to ask for feedback at a later date. This provides you with a valuable 'hook' for future contact and ensures you leave the door open even if you're rejected.

10 top morale boosters

You really can boost your self-esteem and self-confidence if you follow a few simple rules:

1. **List the achievements** you're proud of and collect evidence of success, such as awards, certificates, letters and commendations (go back regularly and check on the skills identified in **Tactic 1**).

2. **Seek feedback.** Add to this list by asking friends, family and colleagues to each name five positive things about you. Yes, it sounds embarrassing, but you'll be surprised at the good things you can learn about yourself – valuable qualities you probably never knew you had. Once you recognise these, you can start to use them to help you. Also, ask people for constructive comments on areas you need to develop. But never take criticism personally.

3. **Update your list of achievements** and positive points regularly and refer to it frequently. This reinforces the good feelings about yourself. Keep a diary of positive events in your life.

4. **Create positive pictures of your world** and the part you play in it. Avoid negative or cynical imagery. You'll build confidence if you exercise your best skills.

5. **Put things in perspective.** Volunteer to support an individual or group who have to cope with far greater challenges than yourself. Also remember that many of the people who appear loud and self-confident on the surface are often quite fragile underneath.

6 **Step beyond your comfort zone** and try new things – anything from a new activity to talking to new people. There's no need to take huge risks – a number of small ones is just as effective (eg give small presentations).

7 **Hang out with positive people.** Build your own support network (see **Tactic 6**) and avoid negative people – they only drag you down to their level.

8 **Learn from other confident people** and invest in a self-development book or course. Recognise that everyone has problems with self-confidence.

9 **Understand why you are rejected.** A job may have been earmarked for an internal candidate. You could be overqualified, not quite the right personality, or someone else has 10 years more experience. Accept that by selecting you for interview, employers have already recognised that your skills and qualities are suitable for the position. It's probably just a matter of time and persistence before you find the right opportunity.

10 **Accept rejection** – it happens to us all and is not that unusual. Learn to accept critical feedback and improve on whatever let you down.

Action prompts

SELLING YOURSELF ON PAPER – YOUR CV

Review your CV in the light of *Creating a CV that sells*.
Also, update it (using that checklist) every time you send it out.

Tick every box honestly.

Spot the gaps and improvements needed.

Keep reviewing the CV – it's an active, ongoing process.

Remember – the checklist maximises your chances of success by taking a client-focused approach. It helps you adapt your CV to meet their needs – not yours!

SELLING YOURSELF IN PERSON

Make sure you use every opportunity for practice using the ideas in *10 top tips to communicate better* (page 40).
Then choose three of the ten ways to create a practical project over a six-month period. Make sure you get feedback on your progress, measure your performance and certainly don't worry about the times you fail.

SELLING YOURSELF AT INTERVIEW

Remember that you need to know just what the person opposite is looking for, so every time you go for an interview:

- Refresh your knowledge of the *20 toughest questions*

- Complete *Your interview checklist* (page 41)

- Predict and rehearse the answers to key questions

KEEPING YOUR EGO IN SHAPE

Use *Your top ten morale boosters* (page 44) to set yourself a mini-project entitled 'Creating my own self-confidence'.
Make sure you work seriously on at least three of the tips.

See this as an ongoing improvement process that never ends.

Read through your lists of positive points before any application or interview. Never undersell your successes.

the art of action thinking

TACTIC

T5

TACTIC FIVE

successful people rarely get where they are by following a pre-planned career — they position themselves to seize future opportunities

The art of action thinking

You've now learned to use some of the Tactics that bring career success.

Tactic 5 **– reveals perhaps the most important one of all** – *action thinking.*

You will find out about:

- **The dynamic process of** *action thinking*

- **Setting short, medium and long-term goals.**

- **The eight steps of** *action thinking*

POSITIONING YOURSELF FOR SUCCESS...

Successful people rarely get where they are by following a pre-planned career path with every step foreseen in advance.

Life just isn't like that. And such a plan is even more unlikely to work in today's fast-changing world of work.

In the real world, success has always been related to:

- Being driven by a strong sense of purpose

- Spotting and seizing opportunities

- Thinking creatively about the next moves ahead

- Creating potentially beneficial chance events

- Making effective use of networking

Action thinking **is the dynamic process of positioning yourself to anticipate and seize future opportunities.** At the same time, it shows you how to create 'chance' events yourself that can give your career a vital boost.

Action thinking **is designed to let you make the most of opportunities in the medium and long term.**

It even makes you ready and able to take advantage of those unpredictable turns life can take.

Of course you still need to plan. Just like conventional action planning, *action thinking* involves regularly setting and reviewing short, medium and long-term goals.

But it's a far more dynamic, flexible and responsive process – and will ensure you develop your career on your terms – nobody else's.

The eight steps to action thinking are designed to help you develop this kind of approach and put it to work.

DEVELOPING YOUR ACTION THINKING

You'll then have the mental attitude that will let you spot – and seize – those big opportunities when they come along.

The next page explains *The eight steps to action thinking*.

Remember the art is to *think* a couple of moves ahead, say two or three years, and:

- **Paint a picture** of how you see your career progressing and sketch a profile of your ideal job as it evolves (see **Tactic 2**)

- **Predict the key skills** and experiences you'll need to enhance your personal development and stay employable (see **Tactic 1**)

- **Look at ways** of maximising your chances of success (**Tactics 3** and **4**)

- *Think* **more strategically** about other networks and opportunities on your doorstep

You then need to *act* by developing your own personal action prompts based on these needs.

Here are some typical questions you need to ask:

- How can I be **more responsive** and seize opportunities?

- What can I do to be **more proactive** and move forward?

- How can I build my **self-confidence** to tackle the potentially daunting tasks ahead?

- How can I look ahead to potential **career moves?**

- Are there any **novel ways** of creating my own career path?

- How am I going to **continue to learn,** network and develop new skills?

- How am I going to **make sure** I'm heading in the right direction?

- How will I stay **responsive** to changing market needs?

- How am I going to **measure** my success in the long term?

TRY THIS...
Get a special perspective for *action thinking* – imagine you're in a helicopter. From the air you can see a long way ahead. You're ideally placed to think about both the medium and long term. But you're also perfectly positioned to zoom down and focus in on any opportunity just ahead that could lead to your eventual destination Try thinking this way all the time – it soon becomes automatic.

The eight steps to action thinking

Step 1 – Identify your overall goal

Try to pinpoint the target you're aiming at and understand what drives you. It's not vital to focus on a precise job – the main thing is to understand the kind of success you want and identify the direction you need to take.

For example, this might be:

Short-term – to secure a new job as an IT trainer within three months.

Medium-term – to explore opportunities of setting up my own small IT training consultancy.

Long-term – to be remembered for creating an innovative IT product within the education field.

Step 2 – Set **SMART** objectives

Map out ways of targeting your actions to achieve the key objectives that will help you reach your goal.

Avoid being vague by making your objectives **SMART** – Specific, Measurable, offering Advantages, Realistic, and with a Timescale.

Make sure you're SMART (page 52).

Step 3 – Take bite-sized chunks

Your objectives may seem daunting at first. Make it easier by breaking them down into manageable chunks. Eg if aiming to gain improved career focus in personnel or marketing, aim to:

- Contact IPD and CIM (professional bodies)
- Read professional journals
- Identify 20 local companies and write for information
- Seek four advisory interviews with friends and contacts

Step 4 – Understand the challenges ahead

We all have traits that stop us developing new skills or experience. Some people are too bitter or negative to do anything – some are simply couch potatoes who basically can't be bothered and others may just lack the vital degree of self-promotion, assertiveness or self-confidence.

The first positive step is to understand what stops you achieving your goals. Consider these typical problems and how the strategies could work for you.

Get rid of the words *can't, won't, don't* and replace them with *can, will, do.*

To *think* about this, *read* **10 problems you can beat** (page 53).

Step 5 – Find help

Pinpoint key people, and identify how they can help you achieve your objectives (see **Tactic 6**). For example:

My sister Kathryn who can give me **encouragement** and a general kick up the backside.

My old lecturer who has **contacts** in the field.

John, a friend of the family who is an experienced personnel manager who can give me **advice.**

Step 6 – Map out opportunities and resources

Think creatively about all opportunities and resources available to you at work, socially, within the community and through further learning (see **Tactic 6**). You could obtain a career development loan and invest in a short IT course – or make the most of local community-based training programmes.

Step 7 – Create realistic timescales

Assign a completion date to every objective and task. Start by setting loads of easily achievable targets (it's always rewarding ticking off the list) – then try to stretch yourself. It's amazing what you can achieve if you simply set yourself challenging targets. You may want to set daily, weekly, monthly, quarterly or yearly targets.

Step 8 – Review your progress

Against your identified targets, measure progress, review your learning from experiences, good and bad, keep your action thinking alive. Learning is a continuous process.

The way to do this is to keep a log, recording key outcomes at each stage of the learning cycle.

4. **PLANNING**
[planning the next steps]

**THE
LEARNING
CYCLE**

2. **REVIEWING**
[reflecting on the experience]

1. **DOING**
[having an experience]

3. **IMPROVING**
[learning lessons and considering improvements]

The learning cycle

Make sure you're **SMART**

This will show you how to map out the key objectives that must be met to achieve your goal. We're often too vague with our objectives, so try to be SMART

SPECIFIC	Make sure the objective has a specific meaning and focus
MEASURABLE	Make sure the objective is measurable
ADVANTAGES	What's in it for me?
REALISTIC	How realistic is it?
TIMESCALE	When will the objective be achieved?

These objectives may relate to:

Developing new skills

Eg: to become self-sufficient in specialist IT and office management systems within the next three months.

Exploring new opportunities

Eg: to seek six advisory interviews with personnel managers in the retail sector within the next two months.

Increasing self-awareness

Eg: to gain feedback from eight friends and peers on their perceptions of my strengths and areas for development. Target date 24 July this year.

Improving self-promotion

Eg: to volunteer to make at least three presentations with the sales team by Christmas and gain feedback on my performance.

Boosting self-confidence

Eg: to spend this Friday afternoon listing my key achievements and skills gained over the past five years.

Gaining career focus

Eg: to spend three hours a week researching career opportunities within training and marketing over the next month and to narrow my options down to one or two key areas.

10 problems you can beat

Once you understand the problems that often stop you from achieving your goals, it's much easier to make these strategies work for you.

LAZINESS	Set yourself regular, short-term tasks. Concentrate on achieving an early success. Make your first attempts easy and achievable. Get someone to help – friend, colleague or family member.
LACKING SELF-CONFIDENCE	Seek positive feedback. Try to stretch yourself. Look for safe opportunities to try new things out. Try an assertiveness course. Take active steps to boost your self-confidence. Don't undersell yourself. Ensure you have a clear focus and review your current performance.
FEAR OF FAILURE OR REJECTION	Learn from your failures as well as successes. Understand rejection is a regular occurrence. Don't take it personally. Major negative incidents are often catalysts for positive change in the medium/long term.
POOR TIME MANAGEMENT	Look at your major time-stealers and see how they can be reduced. Give yourself realistic time each week to achieve your objectives. Allow time for reflection. Have a clear action plan. Prioritise.
NO FOCUS OR DIRECTION	Start by increasing your self-awareness. This takes some time, and you may need to find a helping hand. Try lots of different experiences and eliminate the ones you dislike. Keep open-minded and flexible, but over time try to focus your thoughts.
COMFORT ZONE	Recognise we all have our own comfort zone, a pattern of behaviour in which we feel relaxed. When you stop learning new things in your job, it may be time to move on. Try continually to stretch yourself by volunteering for presentations, taking on new positions or setting up something from scratch.
LACK OF RELEVANT EXPERIENCE	Identify where your gaps are. Find activities to fill them – paid, voluntary, or projects. Creatively explore all options and seize opportunities. Apply your skills in different contexts.
MOTIVATION	Find out what really motivates you. It's also just as important to find and discard things that de-motivate you. You certainly don't want to spend the next 40 years in a job you hate. Try out as many things as early as possible in your career, and give yourself regular rewards.
LIMITED TIME/SUPPORT	Build your own support network. Try to work in teams as well as by yourself. Get a mentor. Recognise the signs of a career rut – 'I'm too busy', 'Too many other important things to think about'.
SCARED OF TAKING RISKS	Don't worry about making the wrong decisions, you may have to test different options out before finding the ideal one. Be aware of the inertia stopping you moving forward – 'It's all I know', 'It's what I'm comfortable with' (job security, support mechanisms, colleagues, benefits package, company culture) – but also be true to yourself.

Action prompts

Use the following prompts to develop the art of *action thinking*

1 **Look at ways** to make yourself more employable and boost your career over the next two to three years.

2 **Refer back to Tactics 1-4** to see how you could move forward.

3 **Draw up** a list of resulting actions.

4 **Use the list** to identify and prioritise short, medium and/or long-term objectives.

5 **Decide** action prompts for each objective using the eight-step approach set out below.

6 **Set SMART objectives** (go to page 52) to achieve each goal.

- *Remember* to keep a record of your ideas and log of your learning

- *Make sure* you revisit and revise your plans after reading the rest of this book

PEOPLE WHO CAN HELP ME ARE

OTHER OPPORTUNITIES & RESOURCES AVAILABLE TO ME ARE

MY TIMESCALES FOR ACHIEVING PARTICULAR TASKS ARE

I'LL KNOW WHEN I'VE GOT THERE WHEN
Outcomes to measure my performance against

WHAT I WANT TO ACHIEVE IS
My overall Aim

I PLAN TO GET THERE BY
My SMART career and learning objectives are

THE STEPS I NEED TO PUT INTO PLACE

CHALLENGES I MAY FACE
Obstacles that might hinder me and ways I will tackle them

giving your
career
a boost

TACTIC

T6

SIX

in **today's** world of
work it's vital that **you**
make the most of
every opportunity

Giving your career a boost

This *Tactic* reveals the three special routes which you can use to reach your goal faster:

- **Making your job work for you**
- **Thinking laterally – the BEST way**
- **Getting a little help from your friends**

In **Tactic 5** you found out about the powerful art of *action thinking*. And by now you should also have some action prompts jotted down as reminders. Don't worry if your ideas sound a bit vague – it's having a start that counts.

In any case, you'll be modifying them all the time as you go along. You should now keep *action thinking* in mind all the time.

Remember, everyone you meet, everything you *read* and everything you do has the potential to reveal a hidden opportunity that could help to modify your *action thinking* a little.

You can no longer simply plod down a neatly signposted pathway knowing you'll reach each career milestone after the prescribed number of years.

Today's career paths are crazy-paved – you have to piece them together yourself using all the imagination and ingenuity at your disposal.

That may seem a problem – but it can also present a big opportunity. If you use these 'short cuts' and apply your *action thinking* effectively, you can progress your career far quicker and more successfully than was ever possible in yesterday's working world.

MAKING YOUR JOB WORK FOR YOU

There's already one terrific opportunity to develop your career right under your nose.

Yes, your place of work. Your present or future job offers endless ways of progressing your career. It's probably the most valuable – and most neglected – opportunity of all.

*We will explain the **10 tips to make your job work for you**.* (page 60) *Remember though, as always, there are no quick fixes – what you put in is what you get out.*

Key points include:

1. **Take** a broader look at your business – map out where the best opportunities lie and how you can reach them (revisit **Tactics 1, 2, 3** and **5**).

2. **Make** a positive impact – identify what you bring to the firm's bottom line and design your own performance improvement project.

3. **Manage** your boss – understand who your real boss is, promote your performance and make the most of his/her experience and contacts.

4. **Show** willingness to develop – volunteer for new roles, join committees and seek development opportunities.

5. **Network** internally and externally – attend courses, conferences etc, and maintain contacts assiduously.

6. **Understand** who holds the power – recognise the people with influence and study how you can raise your profile with them.

7. **Promote** your successes – by creating your own personal marketing plan to influence the people who matter.

8. **Create** time to manage your career – update your CV at least once a year and continually assess ways you can maintain your employability.

9. **Learn** to learn from others – focus on role models, seek guidance and act on feedback.

10. **Improve** continually – check you are adding real value to your organisation, keep learning and regularly review this book.

THINKING LATERALLY - THE *BEST* WAY

Lateral thinking is a further vital technique for moving your career forward quickly.
It's essential to be aware of the opportunities to be found all the time at work, in your social life and within the community and through learning.

In fact, many people fail to develop in their career because they simply lack this ability.

This need never be a problem once you understand the **BEST** way – **B**roaden, **E**njoy, **S**tretch and **T**hink.

BROADEN your horizons – take a wider look at the skills your various interests give you, find useful new ones and cast your net wider for new job openings.

ENJOY what you do – think about what you like doing best and how that can be applied to work opportunities.

STRETCH your potential – work at new skills, try new challenges and take a few risks.

THINK ahead – spot emerging opportunities and position yourself to be in the right place at the right time when one comes your way.

To understand how it pays to think laterally, you need to see the **BEST** technique in action. We've included a range of case studies (page 64) that show how other people have given their careers a boost by remembering to Broaden, Enjoy, Stretch and Think.

GETTING A LITTLE HELP FROM YOUR FRIENDS

There are times when we all need a helping hand, particularly from someone who is both experienced and supportive.

Remember, investing in your career is a long, painstaking process. It's almost impossible to do by yourself. We all need support to grow and develop.

This is why networking is so important. For successful personal development, it's vital to build contacts throughout your working life.

To think about these questions in more depth. go to page 66 – *10 questions that will grow your network*

We all have our role models. But try looking nearer to home – at people you respect and can learn from throughout your career.

The process of finding people who are ready, willing and able to help you is an art in itself and requires specialist skills of a high level.

To make it easier, you need to ask yourself a number of vital questions:

Why do I need a network?
– Everyone offers something different – it may be ideas, skills or friendship and support. The trick is knowing who offers what.

Who can help me?
– Develop a list and you'll be amazed how many people you know and who they can lead to.

What do I want to achieve
– Think clearly how a prospective new member of your network can help you.

How am I going to make contact?
– Networking takes practice so develop the approach that suits you best.

What is the most successful technique?
– 'Information or advisory interviews' are the best way to learn – practise first with friends.

What happens if they say no?
– It happens all the time so accept it, work out why, and keep on learning and trying.

How can I strengthen my network?
– Identify several core members of your network as personal mentors to guide you.

How can I maintain my network?
– Build strong, trusting relationships, help other people, hang around positive people and always keep in touch.

Am I continually growing my network?
– Step out of your comfort zone, take risks, learn new skills and check you're in the right networks.

What are the fundamental ingredients for success?
– Keep on trying and always learn from your mistakes.

10 tips to make your

Your place of work offers endless opportunities for developing your career.

Don' t be daunted by this list of suggestions – you don't need to work your way through it.

Just consider a few you could try – any single one could hold the key to moving your career on.

 Take a broader look at your business

Learn to think of the needs of your whole organisation, not just your job. Gather **market intelligence** to create new openings – it also helps you cope with change and uncertainty.

Carry out your own **mini-research project** to discover:

- Your organisation's priorities over the next few years
- The growth areas
- How customer needs are changing
- New markets and competitors
- The priorities of other departments
- New products or processes
- New skills required

Select the best opportunities and plan how to reach them (revisit **Tactics 1, 2, 3** and **5**).

 Make a positive impact

Decide where you **add greatest value** to your organisation's bottom line.

This could be by:

- Simply freeing up your manager's time (often the simplest way)
- Identifying new markets
- Increasing the sales or customer base/fundraising
- Increasing productivity/improving delivery
- Improving administrative /quality/IT systems
- Developing new products

Always remember you're only as good as your last job

Make yourself **indispensable** in some way.

Set your own 3/6-month **performance improvement** project.

Use this to make a real mark on the business.

 Manage your boss

Identify who your **real boss** is (not just your line manager). Be clear of what is expected of you and how your performance is measured – and make sure it's linked to (1) and (2).

If a regular **performance review system** is not in place, create one yourself.

Understand the agenda of your bosses and their personal strengths and weaknesses.

Work out how they prefer to **communicate** (eg, chats, formal reports, e-mail) and gain regular feedback. Make the most of your own boss's **experience and contacts** and always leave any job or project on a positive note (however bad the experience) – you never know when you'll need a reference.

 Show willingness to develop

Volunteer for **new projects or roles** outside your remit. Get involved in key **committees** or groups. Work across departments and try to learn from people. Explore opportunities across your **whole organisation** and look for secondments or project-based links. Contact managers in other departments, use their experiences and **offer your services**. Make sure your boss knows your development needs – and make it clear if they're not being met.

 Network internally and externally

Use every opportunity to build **new relationships.** Clients, suppliers, distributors, competitors, colleagues and organisations in related fields are all potential avenues for future career moves. Courses, conferences, trade fairs, professional associations, journals, meetings and correspondence are all useful ways to **grow your network.**

Keep an up-to-date **diary** of key contacts. If you leave, **maintain links** with these key contacts via the occasional phone call, e-mail, letter or Christmas card.

job work for you

6 Understand who holds the power

Survey your organisation's structure and list the key names. Understand who holds the **power,** influence and authority. Who dictates the finances? Who has specialist skills? Who knows everything that's going on? **Build relationships** with these key individuals to maximise your **profile and impact.** Be aware of the different political animals – the wise owls, clever foxes, slippery snakes and cunning sharks. But avoid immersing yourself in office politics – it saps your time and energy.

7 Promote your successes

If you don't promote yourself, who else will? Make sure you use every opportunity to **sell your successes** to the people who matter – your internal and external clients (boss, boss's boss, key contacts), understand their agendas and go with the flow.

Learn from highly regarded people. How do they promote themselves? How do they hold people's respect and attention and get their message across? Make sure you are portraying the right kind of image to your colleagues, boss and clients at all times.

Don't undersell yourself. Collect evidence of your achievements such as positive feedback, letters of commendation or certificates. Ask your employers for a reference before you leave, when your contribution is fresh in their minds.

8 Create time to manage your career

Keep **thinking** about the achievements and skills you've gained – and **update** your CV at least once a year. Continually scan the job market and assess ways you can maintain your employability. Explore two new **career opportunities** each year as a reality check to assess whether you're on the right career track.

Invest at least a week's wages every year in developing your career.

Set yourself a new career **project** each year and keep a log of your learning (both good and bad experiences). Look at gaining professional qualifications and focus on developing skills that are transferable in the job market such as IT.

9 Learn to learn from others

Find at least two role models in your organisation or profession that you can learn from.

Look at their career paths, successes and mistakes and relate them to yourself. Identify and learn from people who are competent in skill areas where you're weak and need help (eg excellent presenters, capable managers, good networkers). Find your 'critical friends' – people you respect and trust and ensure you gain regular feedback and guidance from them. Above all, learn to accept critical feedback and act on it!

10 Continually improve

Devote lots of time to reflecting on your progress.

- Are you adding real value to your organisation?
- Are you still learning new things?
- Are you happy in your current role?
- Is your contribution being recognised?
- Are you heading down the right career path?
- Are you regularly reviewing this book?

If the answer to any of these questions is NO – it's time to *act*.

Take ownership of your own development before someone else takes ownership of you.

Moving your career forward

Just one small step…

Nikki finds a new approach

When Nikki's immediate manager failed to recognise her talents, she began to volunteer for small projects in related departments and developed a working relationship with two senior managers.

By discreetly selling her achievements, she raised her profile to the point where she came to mind when they needed to make an internal promotion six months later.

Christine changes her role

Christine felt vaguely dissatisfied with her limited role in the police force which involved redirecting 999 calls.

By giving up a night out each week to attend a career development course, she gained feedback that proved the problem was not the police force but the failure to use her skills.

Through exploring internal career opportunities in administration and customer service, she has given her career a new lease of life.

Tony takes a risk

Tony felt safe in his rut as a small cog in a large firm and was afraid to take risks. However his work of auditing training suppliers had allowed him to develop a good working relationship with an expanding business.

When the supplier mentioned he had a staffing problem, Tony offered his services – much to his own surprise.

He now runs the supplier's small financial section and his career has never looked back.

Kate's story

Kate hated her work and in desperation took Friday afternoons off for jobhunting. Lacking real focus, a couple of rejections led to her wasting this precious time at the hairdressers, shops or pub.

Then a friend made her wake up her ideas and structure her search for work. Kate began to look for feedback on the rejections and was eventually offered an outstanding opening. Her new employer singled out Kate's detailed research on the firm as the factor that made her stand out.

Sue gains a skill boost

As an assistant secretary, Sue lacked self-confidence and was going nowhere fast – until she discovered an interest in IT. Encouraged by staff needing her special skills, she rapidly developed expertise in computer graphics.

Positive feedback from colleagues encouraged her to go for a customer service qualification, and she is now the most valuable member of the team.

Sharon spots a niche

Marketing work for a health foods company together with a spare-time interest in network marketing gave Sharon a unique combination of skills.

Needing a change, she contacted her previous boss who had set up his own health product business.

She quickly spotted a niche market in remedies for eating disorders in the elderly and sold him the idea She now leads a sales team that uses a network approach to product marketing.

The lesson of the two teachers…

Alex anticipated the changes in the National Curriculum and responded by planning new teaching techniques 12 months in advance. She has since been promoted

Martin, her colleague, waited until the changes landed on his desk. Not surprisingly, he is now struggling just to hold down his job.

Dan sees an opportunity

Although unemployed, Dan kept alert to work trends and identified increasing opportunities in healthcare for the elderly.

Some low-level work experience helped to rebuild his self-confidence and develop his expertise.

He then used his new work network to gain a full-time position. He soon identified a gap in the market and created his own job as an assistant healthcare manager.

How to think laterally – the BEST way

BROADEN

- Take a wider look at the portfolio of skills you've gained through voluntary, community, social and part-time work.

- Be creative, and use projects, secondments, part-time vacancies and on-the-job training to create opportunities where traditional career paths don't exist.

- Enrol on a new course, learn a new profession, start a new hobby or make use of a career development loan.

- Continually scan the broader employment market. Stay positive. Work-shadow friends, neighbours and colleagues. Explore a couple of new career options each year and cast your net wider.

ENJOY

- Continually assess whether your job is what you're good at and really enjoy.

- Look at extending things you enjoy doing - eg turning a hobby into a business. Consider moving jobs to use your skills.

- Spend time pinpointing the skills you really enjoy using. Look at how you can create or negotiate more time in these areas.

- Free yourself up to enjoy more quality time. List all the positive things you would like to achieve over the next year.

STRETCH

- Identify a new skill or experience that will enhance your employability and set yourself demanding short-term targets.

- Become a better risk-taker. If you see a gap in the market, go for it. Be prepared to seize opportunities traditionally out of your reach.

- Set yourself regular personal performance plans. Put yourself into new positions of responsibility and challenge. Try out new things and recognise that when you stop learning new things at work it may be time to move on.

- Find a partner or friends who are interested in your career, share the same values and goals, and are prepared to push and support you.

THINK

- Always think a couple of moves ahead. Look at how your profession is changing, highlight the emerging opportunities and learn to spot future growth areas.

- Develop the art of positioning yourself to be 'in the right place at the right time'.

  Get yourself onto key decision-making committees. Connect to the right networks, build the right relationships and invest in developing long-term trust rather than focusing on short-term gains.

- Think of yourself sitting in your rocking chair looking back at your life. Build a picture of all the achievements you would be proud of and like to be remembered for.

- Think smart financially. Get some independent financial advice, consider your pension and investment plans early in your career and invest in your most important asset – yourself.

BEST in action

To help you understand how the BEST technique could work for you, it's worth thinking about these typical case studies:

BEST at WORK

BROADEN

Catriona, administrator for the Chiropody Society

Catriona expanded her fairly narrow role by volunteering to promote the society's work at exhibitions. This raised her profile in the foot care industry. Six months later, the sales manager for an instrument company was so impressed by her promotional skills he head-hunted her onto his field sales team.

ENJOY

Colin, quantity surveyor

Colin had reached a plateau in his role when an internal short-term secondment in marketing arose. He soon realised he enjoyed the creative and people-orientated role far more than his previous technically-based position. He turned it into a full-time position by selling the business benefits of his new role to the Marketing Director.

STRETCH

Eunan, designer for a medium-sized corporate PR company

Eunan didn't fit happily with the organisation's culture of long days and 100% commitment, with little reciprocal reward. With two young children, it would have been all too easy to continue in his comfort zone created by steady pay and security. He took the risk of setting up his own successful design consultancy and the personal rewards have been enormous.

THINK

Bruce, unemployed entrepreneur

Having seen his first market research business go into liquidation, Bruce spent six months unemployed. Realising he couldn't really stand working for anyone else, he looked strategically at the market and identified the telecommunications industry as a major growth area. He now offers specialist market research for major telecoms blue chips and employs six freelance staff.

BEST in the COMMUNITY

BROADEN

Ronnie, former docks industry worker

Forced to leave the industry by new technology and containerisation, Ronnie realised ten years voluntary work with a local community group provided his CV with greater transferable skills and experience than his paid work. A job as a part-time care assistant acted as a stepping stone to team leader managing three care homes.

ENJOY

Helen, clerical officer

When Helen volunteered to help a social club for adults with learning difficulties, she realised she enjoyed helping people to develop far more than the 9-5 desk-bound job she had held for ten years. Encouraged by other club helpers, she enrolled on a diploma in career guidance and is now a highly regarded careers officer dealing with challenging youngsters.

STRETCH

Jane, engineering graduate

After four years volunteering, Jane decided to put herself forward as leader of a local community group. Making announcements to the 70 helpers and members greatly developed her presentation skills and self-confidence, and these assets now form the basis of her work as trainer and adviser to government agencies on employment issues.

THINK

Steff, personnel assistant

Steff reached her ideal job as Training Director for VSO (Voluntary Services Overseas) by developing a balanced portfolio of commercial training and management experience and gaining extensive voluntary experience at home and abroad.

BEST SOCIALLY

BROADEN

James, painter/decorator

James's career was drifting away until he overheard a friend discussing his job in an adult training centre. James asked for an opportunity to work-shadow and it turned into a six-month placement and has now resulted in a permanent job. This showed it can often be who you know – not what you know – that counts.

ENJOY

Tommy, part-time bar worker

Tommy was basically under-employed for two years but the pub job led to an interest in the catering and entertainment industry – particularly corporate hospitality. He formed a partnership with a friend and after naively spending the first six months waiting for the phone to ring, they've now taken a far more proactive, businesslike approach. They may not end up millionaires but now they're paid for their hobby.

STRETCH

Alison, administrative assistant

Looking for a new challenge, Alison turned to her social network of contacts and spoke to a colleague who was interested in personal development issues. She referred Alison to a local career development workshop which helped move her career up a gear and she is now focusing on using her administration, planning and organisational skills in the events-organising industry.

THINK

Sara, commercial manager in retailing

With her children growing up, Sara reviewed her balance between work and time for the family. Her values had also changed, and she was no longer motivated by increasing sales of ladieswear by another 20%. Although it's a major risk, she has joined a smaller company on a one-year contract at much less pay. Things are now in place to get the balance right.

BEST in LEARNING

BROADEN

Peter, economic development officer

Peter adopts the supermarket approach to career development – every internal or external training course goes into his shopping trolley. He keeps a totally open mind on the basis that you never know where it will lead and when you may need it. His latest 'purchase' (for which, as always, his company is paying) is a web page designer's course.

ENJOY

Sue, researcher for BBC Radio.

While running a health documentary Sue rekindled her lifelong interest in dentistry. Enrolling as a mature student, and paying her fees by working as an evening receptionist at her local BBC Radio station, she recently qualified after five years of hard graft. The key to success was finding something she really enjoyed, and being totally committed and persistent.

STRETCH

Mary, marketing manager

Mary has no great career aspirations but is keenly aware of the need to stay flexible and adaptable in a continually changing workplace. She's embarked on the CIM (Chartered Institute of Marketing) professional qualification which gives her a recognised, transferable qualification and opens up numerous learning networks.

THINK

Ian, history graduate

To work in the aircraft industry , Ian had to take four career leaps. After two years providing administrative support in the technical services unit of a boilermaking company, he managed to be seconded onto the design and new product development team where he learned his trade on the job. He then used his design skills to move to a supplier of braking equipment for the aircraft industry, moving finally into quality control with a well-known company.

10 questions that will grow your network

1. WHY DO I NEED A NETWORK?

We all need different types of support. When establishing a particular element of your network you need clearly to define its purpose and content. Always set yourself clear objectives, eg:

- **To find out** about a career in the media by talking to a family friend in local broadcasting

- **To improve** your presentation skills by looking at the attributes of three good presenters

- **To get advice** on your CV from someone already in the job you're seeking

Identify a few people you consider good networkers.
Find out why – and how – they operate.

2. WHO CAN HELP ME?

It's amazing how many useful people you know already – and how many they know.

- **List all** your family and friends, colleagues and other contacts. What do they do for a living? Are they in jobs you would like? What help have they given before? How can they help now?

- **Think creatively** about past and present contacts such as old lecturers, classmates, drinking pals, social friends, neighbours and friends

- **If they can't help,** ask if they know someone else who can

- **Revisit** your diary and telephone book to spark off new ideas

- **Add** to the list by thinking of people who have been recommended by friends, people you've read about, heard of etc

- **Keep** your list up to date

- **Look** at every opportunity to make new contacts

- **Remember,** the right people (those who can make a difference to your career) come in many different guises, so always keep on the look-out

3. WHAT DO I WANT TO ACHIEVE?

Having selected someone to form part of your network, start with the end in mind. Think about what you want the outcome of the meeting to be (see 1).

- **Start by** thinking how they benefit from speaking to you (eg massage their ego, help them reflect, provide reciprocal support, enable them to pass on their learning, gain access to new networks, help with their continuing professional development)

- **Find out** as much about their background and agenda as possible

- **Use all** your contacts for market research – secretaries, colleagues, friends of friends

- **Map out** the key questions (depending on your objective),eg:

  - Can you describe your current role?

  - How have you reached your current position?

  - What skills, qualifications and experience are vital for your position?

  - What are the main lessons you've learned?

  - Would you have done anything differently?

  - What advice would you give me on ....?

  - How is your profession changing?

  - If you were faced with 'situation X' what would you do?

  - I have an idea/problem with 'X'. What's your advice?

  - Is there anybody else it might be useful to speak to?

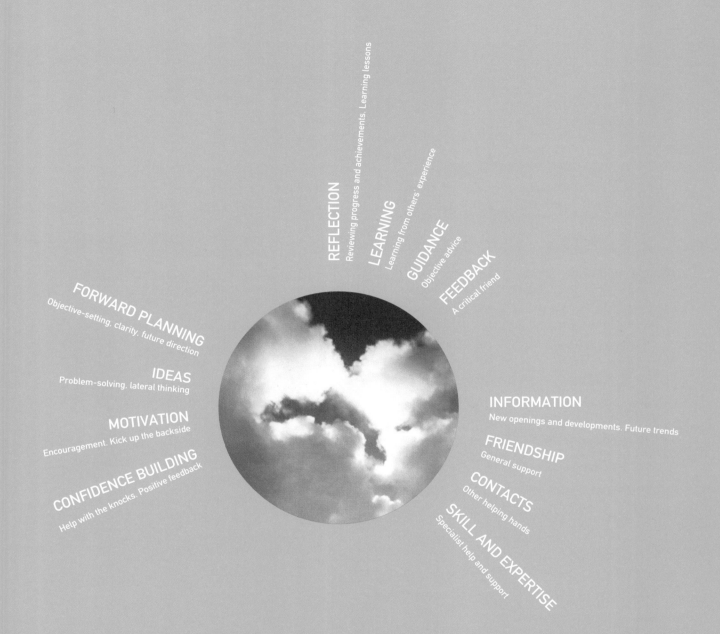

REFLECTION
Reviewing progress and achievements. Learning lessons

LEARNING
Learning from others' experience

GUIDANCE
Objective advice

FEEDBACK
A critical friend

FORWARD PLANNING
Objective-setting, clarity, future direction

IDEAS
Problem-solving, lateral thinking

MOTIVATION
Encouragement. Kick up the backside

CONFIDENCE BUILDING
Help with the knocks. Positive feedback

INFORMATION
New openings and developments. Future trends

FRIENDSHIP
General support

CONTACTS
Other helping hands

SKILL AND EXPERTISE
Specialist help and support

Network benefits

4. HOW AM I GOING TO MAKE CONTACT?

Networking is a skill in itself and requires lots of practice. Start simply in non-threatening situations. Use informal opportunities more than formal meetings:

- **Have a clear agenda:** 'I would like to find out about opportunities in personnel'

- **Obtain a referral** from someone who knows both you and them where possible: 'James suggested I spoke to you'

- **Use flattery,** but don't go overboard: 'You're an ideal person to speak to as you're at the leading edge of the field'

- **Be professional** and efficient: 'I'll only take up 20 minutes of your time'

- **Show appreciation:** 'I would really value your input'

- **Always keep an open door:** 'I realise you're really busy at the moment. Could I contact you in a couple of weeks?'

- **Use whatever approach is most comfortable.** We don't all have to be extroverts. Use letters, fax or e-mail if you're not ready to meet face-to-face

5. WHAT IS THE MOST SUCCESSFUL TECHNIQUE?

An **information or advisory interview** is an ideal way to get to know people and learn from them.

Before the meeting:

- **Ensure** you've mapped out all your key questions

- **Rehearse** by asking friends and colleagues to check the content/order of your questions

During the meeting:

- **Be enthusiastic** and professional – a positive attitude, appearance and manner is crucial

- **Ask open-ended** (rather than yes/no questions), listen actively and show a keen interest

- **Be quick on your feet** – ask probing questions and learn to spot opportunities

- **Keep a log** of the main points arising

- **Offer thanks**

After the meeting:

- **Follow** up your meeting (letter, phone, e-mail, fax) to thank them, remind them of your existence, show interest and indicate you'd like to keep in touch

- **Use the information** you've gained at forthcoming meetings. 'That's interesting because ...'

- **Learn** from the experience – how can I improve my technique? What new leads need following up? How will I change my approach next time?

6. WHAT HAPPENS IF THEY SAY NO?

- Always have a **positive attitude,** the worst thing they can say is no

- Be realistic, you're going to get rejected more times than you're accepted

- Understand why you failed first time around, and address it

- Don't take rejection **personally** – most successful people are busy and in demand

- Spend time with **positive** people – they'll keep you going

- Always look for **additional opportunities** 'As you're so busy, perhaps you could suggest someone else?'

- **Be persistent.** Really important people may need half-a-dozen different attempts

THE 5 I'S OF RELATIONSHIP-BUILDING

INITIATE
Always be proactive
INFORM
Target your messages
INFLUENCE
Build confidence in your judgement
IMPACT
Make it a win-win relationship
IMPROVE
Continue to grow trust

7. HOW CAN I STRENGTHEN MY NETWORK?

It's important to identify several core members –
personal mentors or coaches who can guide and support you.
These are people:

- **You can talk** to honestly and openly about how you feel,
  perhaps a family member, a work colleague, boss,
  friend or partner

- **With a positive attitude** (especially towards you) who will
  build your confidence

- **Who you respect and trust...**

- Who have already followed a similar **career path** and can
  offer **personal experience**

- Who are already where you'd like to be in terms of job,
  lifestyle, **freedom and influence**

- Who are themselves good **networkers**

Don't forget - you'll probably have more than one mentor.

8. HOW CAN I MAINTAIN MY NETWORK?

It's crucial to build robust partnerships and relationships:

- Take time to build **trust,** there are no quick-fix solutions

- Remember it's a **two-way process.** You'll be part of other
  people's networks.

  If you help people too, they'll be more likely to help you

- Make sure you hang around **positive people**

- Always offer thanks and **recognition**

- Dedicate time to simply **keeping in touch** with people as
  their lives change (ring, write, e-mail, visit key contacts
  at regular intervals)

9. AM I CONTINUALLY GROWING MY NETWORK?

It's vital to stretch yourself by stepping out of your comfort zone.

- Take lots of **tiny risks** and contact new people

- Continually develop your **networking skills,** eg telephone
  technique, interpersonal skills, relationship-building

- Access the **gaps** in your personal network –
  find more inspirational people in your field

- Set yourself regular **objectives** – don't stagnate

- Make sure you're really putting **effort** into 1 - 8 above

- Take a hard look at whether you're in the **'right' networks**
  for you

10. WHAT ARE THE FUNDAMENTAL INGREDIENTS FOR SUCCESS?

- Be persistent

- Stay positive

- Accept rejection

- Learn from both your good and bad experiences

- Don't worry if you're not perfect

- Take small steps to improve

Action prompts

THINKING LATERALLY – THE *BEST* WAY

Review the case studies and identify how you can do your **BEST**:

- At work
- Within the community
- Socially
- Through learning

MAKING YOUR JOB WORK FOR YOU

Think about the *10 top tips to make your job work for you* **and identify priority actions you can put into effect at work.**

Once again, don't feel you have to be superperson. Look for small steps you can take to get yourself moving.

GETTING A LITTLE HELP FROM YOUR FRIENDS

1   **Review** your current approach to networking by asking yourself the *10 questions that will grow your network* (page 66) and identifying areas in which you need to improve.

2   **Set** yourself **SMART** objectives (page 52) indicating how you intend to grow your network over the next six months and review your progress.

3   **Return** to your action prompts to see how your network can help you reach your goals.

ACTIONS	PRIORITY	PROGRESS TO DATE	ACTION NEEDED
1 Taking a broader business perspective			
2 Making a positive impact			
3 Managing my boss			
4 Showing a willingness to develop			
5 Networking internally and externally			
6 Understanding who holds the power			
7 Selling my success			
8 Creating time to manage my career			
9 Learning from others			
10 Continual improvement			

measuring your career management performance

TACTIC

T7

SEVEN

you **probably** spend more time **planning** your holiday than your **career**

me ^{plc}

By now, you'll probably have realised how complex this whole process of managing your career is.

You need to be extremely self-reliant.

This involves coping with the changing world around you, taking responsibility for your own career and personal development; and managing the relationship with work and with learning throughout all stages of your life. It's a continuous, lifelong process.

The following section helps you to assess how good you really are at managing your career, and the extent to which you've put the principles of this book into action – it will provide you with a measure of where you are strong and where you need to develop if you are going to improve your career management performance.

A word of warning before you embark on this penultimate exercise – don't worry if your score isn't as high as you would hope.

The important thing is to refer back to the book in areas where your score is low.

The **Performance Audit**, on the following pages, is based on the principle that we are all a business of one – *me plc,* and includes five inter-related sections:

1. Where am I now?
2. Where do I want to be?
3. How do I get there?
4. Getting there.
5. Review and improvement.

Each section has 10 statements. Carefully read through each statement and score yourself on the following basis:

0. Feel that I'm poor and under-developed in this area. It still needs a lot of work.

1. I'm OK at this but I still need to work on it.

2. I'm good or above average at this.

3. I feel confident enough to say that I'm excellent in this area – and I can back up my confidence with clear and current evidence of my achievements.

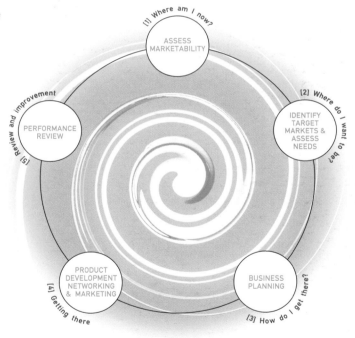

Having completed the **Performance Audit,** total all the individual scores, and refer to the final **'What Next?'** section. Assess your key areas for development and plan to take action! Don't forget, the higher you score the more likely you are to get what you really want from your career.

1. Where am I now?

		POOR	FAIR	GOOD	EXCELLENT
1.1	I am fully aware of my portfolio of skills, experience, knowledge and attributes that makes me stand out in the employment market place	0	1	2	3
1.2	I have an up-to-date, well-organised, concise and accurate CV which clearly sells these strengths	0	1	2	3
1.3	I have comprehensive physical evidence which provides greater details of my personal portfolio (ie Record of Achievement, learning log, client references, examples of major achievements)	0	1	2	3
1.4	I regularly seek feedback from people at all levels regarding my performance. For example, my peers have given me objective feedback on my strengths and areas for development	0	1	2	3
1.5	I maintain regular contact with professionals in my field in order to know how relevant my portfolio of skills and expertise is to my future employability and career goals	0	1	2	3
1.6	I am aware that I have a number of internal and external clients in my current position and continually try to improve my relationship with them	0	1	2	3
1.7	I am clear on my motivations in life and these are closely matched to my current and future plans	0	1	2	3
1.8	I know in which environments I learn most effectively, and make full use of the current range of learning opportunities available to me	0	1	2	3
1.9	I deal with change and uncertainty in a positive, flexible and open-minded manner	0	1	2	3
1.10	I feel good about myself and have underlying self-confidence in my capabilities	0	1	2	3

SUB TOTAL [MAX 30]

2. Where do I want to be?

		POOR	FAIR	GOOD	EXCELLENT
2.1	I know what I want to achieve in my career and have a clear picture of my 'ideal job'	0	1	2	3
2.2	I know what I want to achieve in my personal life	0	1	2	3
2.3	I allow myself enough time to plan my future and regularly set short-term learning and career development objectives	0	1	2	3
2.4	I have creatively explored all the career development opportunities available to me at work, within the community, socially and through learning	0	1	2	3
2.5	I have interviews, by way of advisory discussions, with people in my next job, or next-but-one targeted job or position	0	1	2	3
2.6	I have examined how my current portfolio of skills and experience could be applied to different career options	0	1	2	3
2.7	I know what level and balance of skills and knowledge will be required to progress and grow in my job, my organisation and my area of expertise	0	1	2	3
2.8	I recognise the benefits and limitations of pursuing particular career paths (ie limited jobs in sectors that are in economic decline)	0	1	2	3
2.9	I make the most of my network of contacts for advice and guidance on future career plans	0	1	2	3
2.10	I have made an informed decision on my future career based on a realistic assessment of my core strengths, motivations, experiences, opportunities and constraints	0	1	2	3

SUB TOTAL [MAX 30]

3. How do I get there?

		POOR	FAIR	GOOD	EXCELLENT
3.1	I am prepared to be flexible and adaptable to achieve my long-term goals, and am aware of the different career management options available to me	0	1	2	3
3.2	I have high-level project management skills which apply to managing myself	0	1	2	3
3.3	I continually set myself specific career development objectives with measurable outcomes and written defined timescales. These are committed to paper, but are flexible and reviewed regularly	0	1	2	3
3.4	I break these objectives into practical manageable steps	0	1	2	3
3.5	I have one or more guides or mentors who can help me set realistic plans	0	1	2	3
3.6	I maintain and make effective use of up-to-date labour market intelligence in my field	0	1	2	3
3.7	I have pinpointed the people who can help me achieve my objectives	0	1	2	3
3.8	I have the ability to learn from the successes and mistakes of others	0	1	2	3
3.9	I understand and have the capability to deal with hidden political tensions and power struggles within organisations	0	1	2	3
3.10	I am aware of internal and external factors that can help or hinder me (eg my own limitations or funding decisions out of my control.)	0	1	2	3

SUB TOTAL [MAX 30]

4. Getting there

		POOR	FAIR	GOOD	EXCELLENT
4.1	I am confident at orally promoting the benefits I can bring to a situation (ie good interview and self-presentation skills)	0	1	2	3
4.2	I am able clearly to articulate my strengths through written or visual communication (eg targeted applications, project proposals, creative design)	0	1	2	3
4.3	I have high-level research skills with a proven track record of investigating and creating new opportunities	0	1	2	3
4.4	I am aware of my own comfort zone and actively try to stretch beyond it by taking lots of small risks	0	1	2	3
4.5	I continue to develop and maintain a support network for advice, encouragement, information and help with problem-solving	0	1	2	3
4.6	I have one or more role models, mentors or coaches from whom I can learn from and receive support in my personal and/or professional development	0	1	2	3
4.7	I regularly read journals, newspapers and books, both within my industry and profession and in management and business in general	0	1	2	3
4.8	I manage my time effectively and efficiently, spending the greatest time doing things I enjoy and am good at	0	1	2	3
4.9	I know how to add value and become indispensable in my current (and/or future) organisation	0	1	2	3
4.10	I know what I want to get out of my employer relationship and what I need to put in, and am confident at negotiating the best deal for myself	0	1	2	3

SUB TOTAL [MAX 30]

5. Review & improvement

		POOR	FAIR	GOOD	EXCELLENT
5.1	I regularly review my progress against objectives I set myself, and am able to adjust my goals in the light of changing circumstances	0	1	2	3
5.2	I regularly take dedicated time out to reflect more deeply on my learning	0	1	2	3
5.3	I am aware of when I reach a plateau in my learning and then actively seek new opportunities	0	1	2	3
5.4	I continually assess the balance between my work and personal life	0	1	2	3
5.5	I continue to develop a balanced and flexible portfolio of skills and expertise so that I can be sure of maintaining my future employability	0	1	2	3
5.6	I am able to accept and learn from failure and critical feedback in a positive manner	0	1	2	3
5.7	I maintain an active commitment to lifelong learning (ie I can develop new styles of learning to enhance my flexibility)	0	1	2	3
5.8	I continually seek out external feedback on my performance and learn from both successes and failures	0	1	2	3
5.9	I continually develop my support network to provide me with added security, self-confidence, information, guidance and learning etc	0	1	2	3
5.10	I am able to maintain a feeling of self-worth even in the face of rejection	0	1	2	3

SUB TOTAL [MAX 30]

GRAND TOTAL add all five sub totals [MAX 150]

What next?

This audit provides you with an opportunity to consider your strengths and weaknesses, as expressed through your levels of self-reliance and self-motivation. However, you may also be interested in an overall indication of your performance.

YOUR PERFORMANCE – A ROUGH GUIDE

Don't worry about your score.

Look at three or four areas in your audit where you scored lowest and take steps to address them.

Refer back to the book for help.

Keep coming back to this audit as you plan your future.

		COMMENT	ACTION
A 126-150	COMMENT	You're very focused, aware of your strengths and opportunities, flexible in a changing world and a self-starter with all the hallmarks of a true lifelong learner.	Keep going because what you're doing is not a static process. Make sure you have realistically scored yourself – and be aware of making general assumptions that can't be backed up with evidence. Focus on continual improvement.
B 101-125	COMMENT	You're well on your way to effectively managing your career and lifelong learning.	Take another look at the low scores within your audit. Ensure you understand where the gaps are and develop an Action Plan to address areas for development. Make sure you are using all the resources available to you.
C 70-100	COMMENT	You're doing well, but are you making the most of the opportunities to manage your learning and career?	See A and B. You may also wish to consider: How can I be more proactive? Where are my real obstacles? Do they revolve around time, ability, resources or motivation? Can someone help me develop and reflect on my Action Plan?
D Below 70	COMMENT	You're obviously good in certain areas, and not all statements may be relevant to you. Think carefully about how you can be more proactive, and don't sell yourself short.	See A, B & C above. Like many people you have the capability but you need to work on the consistency of your approach. You may tend to react only in time of trouble, frustration or boredom – and then you probably find yourself ill-equipped to deal with the situation, or you've missed a golden opportunity. Positive steps may include: taking time out for reflection, finding a mentor, building your network and researching future opportunities available to you.

Build WINDMILLS not walls

There is one vital thing this book should have done for you – it should have given you confidence.

You now realise that with the right approach and preparation, we can all take control of the forces shaping our lives and turn them to our advantage.

You now have at your fingertips a set of practical tactics to help you do this.

You know how to identify your special skills – and you've realised you have far more than you thought. You also know how to relate those skills to your ideal job.

You've also learned how to reveal those hidden opportunities and then how to sell yourself to prospective employers.

You know too the shortcuts that can boost your chances – whether by making your present job work for you, by thinking laterally or by making real use of networking.

*And to put these various **Tactics** into practice you have the powerful key **Tactic** of action thinking.*

By now you probably also have a tentative set of action prompts to help you.

So what else do you need to know?

One simple thing. Just keep reminding yourself that managing your career is a full-time job in itself.

And action thinking is the key to success. Spotting those opportunities – and creating them yourself – will keep moving you closer to that ideal job.

And luckily for you, in life you'll find opportunities are always blowing in your direction.

So remember to build windmills....not walls!

Good Luck!

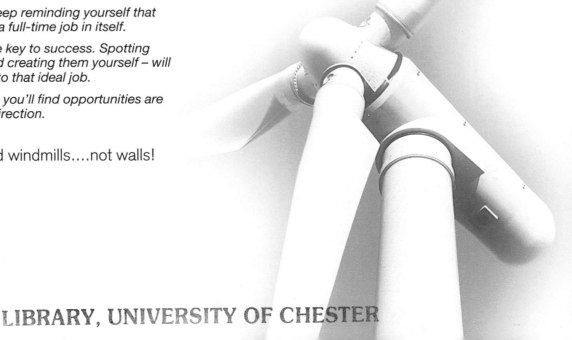